ASTD Trainer's WorkShop Series

Diversity TRAINING

Includes CD-ROM With Ready-to-Use Microsoft PowerPoint™ Presentations

Exercises, Handouts, Assessments, and Tools to Help You:

- ✔ Create Diversity Training That Celebrates Similarities (Conversity®) Rather Than Differences
- ✔ Differentiate Myth From Fact, Get Full Management Support, and Focus on Bottom-Line Performance
- ✔ Become a More Effective and Efficient Facilitator
- ✔ Ensure Training Is on Target and Gets Results

Cris Wildermuth

With Susan Gray

12 11 10 09 08 4 5 6 7 8 9

This publication provides information about diversity training that is crafted to help the user of this book design and develop effective training. This publication and the information contained herein do not constitute legal advice—either the application of law to an individual's or organization's specific circumstances. We strongly recommend you consult with a lawyer if you want professional advice appropriate for you or your organization's particular situation.

ASTD Press is an internationally renowned source of insightful and practical information on workplace learning and performance topics, including training basics, evaluation and return-on-investment (ROI), instructional systems development (ISD), e-learning, leadership, and career development.

Ordering Information: Books published by ASTD Press can be purchased by visiting our Website at store.astd.org or by calling 800.628.2783 or 703.683.8100.

Library of Congress Catalog Card Number: 2004113454

ISBN-10: 1-56286-372-X
ISBN-13: 978-1-56286-372-2

Acquisitions and Development Editor: Mark Morrow

Copyeditor: Christine Cotting, UpperCase Publication Services, Ltd.

Interior Design and Production: UpperCase Publication Services, Ltd.

Cover Design: Ana Ilieva

Cover Illustration: Todd Davidson

Printed by Victor Graphics, Inc. Baltimore, Md.
www.victorgraphics.com

The ASTD Trainer's WorkShop Series

The ASTD Trainer's WorkShop Series is designed to be a practical, hands-on road map to help you quickly develop training in key business areas. Each book in the series offers all the exercises, handouts, assessments, structured experiences, and ready-to-use presentations needed to develop effective training sessions. In addition to easy-to-use icons, each book in the series includes a companion CD-ROM with PowerPoint™ presentations and electronic copies of all supporting material featured in the book.

The Books in the Trainer's Workshop Seriies include:

- ***Coaching Training***
  Chris Chen
- ***Communication Skills Training***
  Maureen Orey and Jenni Prisk
- ***Customer Service Training***
  Maxine Kamin
- ***Diversity Training***
  Cris Wildermuth and Susa Gray
- ***Innovation Training***
  Ruth Ann Hattori and Joyce Wycoff
- ***Leadership Training***
  Lou Russell
- ***Leading Change Training***
  Jeffrey Russell and Linda Russell
- ***New Employee Orientation Training***
  Karen Lawson
- ***New Supervisor Training***
  John Jones and Chris Chen
- ***Project Management Training***
  Bill Shackelford
- ***Sales Training***
  Jim Mikula
- ***Strategic Planning Training***
  Jeffrey Russell and Linda Russell
- ***Teamwork Training***
  Sharon Boller

Contents

Preface

This book is meant to be used as an aid in either developing or enhancing a diversity program. It provides you with a road map for diversity—a combination of business case discussions, research information, and a thorough description of four diversity development sessions.

You will notice that the format for this book is a bit different from that of some others in the Trainer's WorkShop Series. For instance, you won't find the standard sequence of chapters describing one-hour, half-day, one-day, and two-day programs. Another difference is the presence of a leadership presentation that will help you sell the diversity development process internally. Finally, the book includes a fairly detailed background chapter (chapter 3: What Does Science Tell Us About Diversity?).

There are two main reasons for the differences in format. First, diversity development takes time and effort. After all, discrimination is often the result of years of cultural programming. It is impossible to even begin to undo such programming in a single one-hour session.

Second, this is a sensitive topic. Diversity development professionals may face considerable resistance from trainees, and they should consider the legal ramifications of their work. It is possible to make things worse instead of better. Diversity development is not for the fainthearted.

Acknowledgments

Writing a book explaining the basis for our diversity philosophy has been our goal since the beginning of our partnership. When Mark Morrow, ASTD's Manager of Acquisitions and Development, invited us to write the new ASTD diversity manual, we were thrilled. We have both been involved with ASTD for years, so writing a book to be published by ASTD was especially rewarding.

Many wonderful people contributed to this book. Our first thank-you goes to Mark Morrow, for his confidence in our work and for giving us the opportunity to contribute to this useful series of training materials. We are also very grateful to Christine Cotting, our editor, and her superb editing work. Christine was a delight to work with and a tireless advocate for our readers.

We wish to acknowledge our friend Maxine Kamin, author of ASTD's *Customer Service Training* Manual, and the person who connected us to Mark in the first place. Throughout the process, Maxine has been a reader, a friend, and a source of encouragement.

As we finish this project, I (Cris) silently thank my dad, who is no longer with us. Commander Horacio de Mello e Souza was a man with undying integrity and patriotism. He taught me to try harder, aim higher, and never to give up. My mom is an amazing woman—her intelligence, persistence, and quest for learning inspire us all. I need to thank Susan Gray, my business partner and friend, with whom I share most of my waking hours, crazy nights, and impossible deadlines. I also acknowledge, with gratitude, the support Susan and I received from Sandy Bocklett and April Lenhart, and the teachings of two amazing professors at the College of Technology of Bowling Green State University: Dr. Larry Hatch and Dr. Janice Black. My strongest love and gratitude go to my husband Mel, who handles all small and large life emergencies as I discover the virtues of every U.S. airport, work on the Internet until the wee hours, and virtually forget the house exists. Nothing I do could happen without the support I receive at home from Mel and our little daughter, Maggie. You have both shared the writing of this book with us.

My (Susan's) first acknowledgment goes to Cris. Her dad could be very proud of her writing passion, skill, and leadership. It is Cris' intelligence in this area that has propelled this project. Our partnership benefits from her ever-flowing creative talents and her voluminous productivity. Cris is a gift to me and to the world. Kudos go to my sister, Jennifer Shaffer, for nurturing my self-confidence and encouraging me to share my insights. I am very grateful to her for giving me my wings. Valuing others, appreciating differences, and authentic synergy activates my passion, my dad inspired my life's passions through his example and still guides me from above. I continue to look for better solutions, thanks to my mom's modeling. Thanks to professors, mentors, and friends who saw in me what I have learned to see in myself and encouraged me to keep reaching. Finally, my life today owes to those I hold most dear: my husband, David, my son, Christian, and Spud, my 13-year-old dog. It is in the daily living that I remember what really matters most. *Namaste.*

Cris Wildermuth
Susan Gray
December 2004

Chapter 1

Introduction: How to Use This Book Effectively

What's in This Chapter?

- Overview of diversity
- Introduction to Conversity, a process that helps people find connections through dialogue
- Description of the contents of this book
- Explanation of how to use this book effectively

There were never in the world two opinions alike, no more than two hairs or two grains; the most universal quality is diversity.

– Michel Eyquem, Seigneur de Montaigne (1533–1592), French essayist

"Celebrate Diversity!" is the chosen title for many diversity initiatives around the country. The title seems to ring true and make sense. In the global economy of the 21st century, diversity is everywhere. Even if your organization doesn't yet operate internationally, workplace teams are diverse—by definition incorporating differences in dimensions such as talent, personality style, ability, race, gender, age, ethnicity, religion, sexual orientation, and culture.

This chapter is a starting point for the interventions recommended later in the book. Here you will find an overview of diversity, a summary of the topics included in the workbook, and some helpful hints on how to use the materials included most effectively. You will also be introduced to Conversity®, a process that seeks to bring people together though an active search for common ground.

Overview of Diversity

Are you searching for an unemotional and straightforward definition of the word *diversity? Merriam-Webster's Collegiate Dictionary* (10th edition) may offer you one. It defines the word as the condition of being

- unlike
- composed of distinct elements or qualities.

The word *diversity,* however, is anything *but* unemotional. It evokes strong emotional reactions from leaders, practitioners, and people affected by diversity interventions and solutions.

The "what is diversity?" question stirs myriad thoughts and opinions, some positive and others negative. The positive reactions generally come from people who see themselves as able to value, actively invite, and embrace differences. For people in this category, the idea that valuing differences is an important and possible goal is an almost uncontested truth. But uncontested "truths" are often based on a number of equally uncontested assumptions. For instance, it may be assumed that diversity will inevitably improve productivity and bring clear bottom-line benefits. If only it were so easy.

This book began as a how-to manual to help managers, trainers, and diversity practitioners. The initial goal was simply to summarize the most competitive practices in the field and weave them into a well-designed workshop, with a timeline, activity descriptions, and all needed materials. However, research has brought to light some very specific recommendations for anyone designing a diversity training program, and we felt it was important to share this information with our readers. Here are some of those recommendations:

1. Compile a diversity business case that is based on actual research findings, not on rhetoric or emotion.
2. Focus on all aspects of team performance improvement, not merely on prejudice reduction.
3. Recognize that team performance improvement is a long-term process, one that calls for considerable commitment from the entire organization and significant systemic changes. Training is just a piece of that pie.

In addressing diversity relations, it's critical that group members actively search for commonalities and agree on a clearly defined common goal. In the end, the main objective of a *corporate* diversity development system is the unleashing of each person's potential so that there is a positive impact on the organization's bottom line. This may or may not be one's personal goal. For someone concerned with wider societal change, diversity as a bottom-line topic may seem too small and shallow. Many people would rather see their jobs as changing the world because they hope for peace and understanding and a world free of prejudices and barriers. There is nothing wrong with those reasons for embracing diversity. After all, they are the very reasons that draw people into this field. Diversity practitioners and advocates, however, need to understand that improving diversity relations in general is a *societal* goal, not a corporate one. *Corporate* goals should clearly benefit the bottom line of the corporation for which they are designed.

What Is Conversity?

Throughout this book you will see references to *Conversity*. We chose this word to frame diversity initiatives and help participants focus on what they have in common rather than on their differences. Conversity is defined here as *an intentional focus on commonalities leading to attitudes and behaviors that capitalize on human differences for organizational success.* Arguably the word *diversity* does not build support for stronger teams. Specifically, the word *diversity*

- focuses on differences rather than on commonalities
- seems divisive
- carries negative baggage and elicits negative thoughts in some people
- may generate defensiveness and hinder further dialogue.

Conversity, on the other hand, sounds more positive and proactive. Its Latin roots are

- *con*—with, together, for
- *verse*—to familiarize by experience, study, or practice.

Conversity is an active and deliberate search for the kinds of commonalities that bring people together. Even though Conversity is a basis for all interventions, it is not the ultimate goal—that is, synergy and quality. Rather, Conversity is simply the common language that team members need to learn before they are ready to reach their fullest potential. Also of note is the substitution of the words *education* or *educational interventions* for the word *training.* This is an intentional choice. In the field of workplace learning and performance, *training* refers to a single event that could be enriched by a follow-up session.

Education, on the other hand, conjures up images of a long-term process, perhaps life-long. Because diversity development includes long-term behavioral and attitudinal processes, the term *education* makes more sense.

Overview of the Chapters in This Workbook

The connection between diversity and productivity will be decoded in chapter 2: Rewriting the Business Case for Diversity Development. The chapter will differentiate myth from fact in the diversity debate and help you build your own case for improving diversity relations.

Expecting the average person to actively seek and value differences may be unrealistic. In chapter 3: What Does Science Tell Us About Diversity? we will summarize the results of a social psychology literature search. We strongly recommend that you read that chapter carefully because it is the basis for the Conversity philosophy and it provides the rationale for all activities included in later chapters.

Chapters 4, 5, and 6 are practical chapters that help you effectively and efficiently prepare for your training sessions.

Because it is critical in diversity initiatives to have the full support of the organization's top leadership, this book includes a detailed chapter to help you plan and facilitate a leadership kick-off session. In chapter 7 you will find a fully scripted presentation, including PowerPoint slides, to use in seeking leadership's commitment.

Chapters 8, 9, 10, and 11 fully describe four diversity development modules and give you tips, ideas, and detailed agendas using our learning activities, training instruments, and tools. Each module comes complete with step-by-step facilitator instructions and a PowerPoint presentation. The modules are designed to be run in sequence, with each module serving as a prerequisite for the next.

All learning activities are described in chapter 12, and training instruments, assessments, and tools are presented in chapter 13.

How to Use This Workbook

Even though you may be tempted to skip straight to the workshop description and materials, we believe that this book will provide the most benefits if you first familiarize yourself with the business case discussion (chapter 2) and the social psychology review (chapter 3).

We also suggest that you

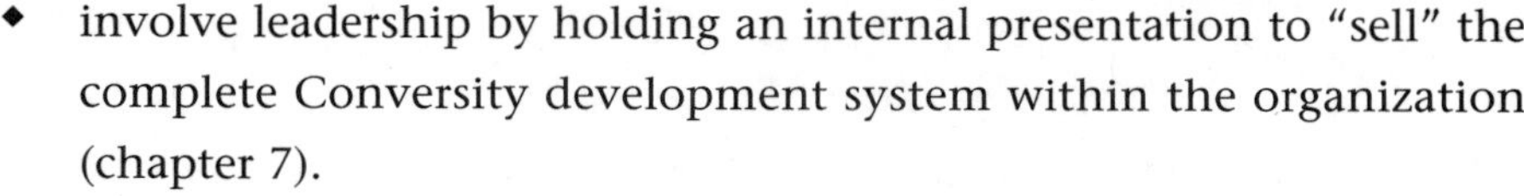

- involve leadership by holding an internal presentation to "sell" the complete Conversity development system within the organization (chapter 7).
- review the diversity development modules (chapters 8–11).
- explore the enclosed PowerPoint presentations and the participant materials included on the accompanying CD-ROM.
- plan pilot programs for each of the modules you decide to run and customize them to your specific business needs.
- use the references listed in the For Further Reading section at the back of the workbook as a starting point for further research.
- develop a comprehensive diversity strategy, including initiatives that go beyond training (for example, recruitment and selection, compensation and rewards, leadership styles, career plans, and other aspects that affect organizational human behavior).

Above all, remember that diversity development is a long-term process, not an event. It won't happen because you conduct a workshop—no matter how good your workshop is. The negative attitudes and feelings that often hinder group processes take generations to develop. Expecting them to be eliminated by a one-time activity makes no more sense than expecting to construct a tall building in a single day. This book will give you a headstart toward deep and meaningful change, but if you are serious about developing your people, it should be just that . . . a start.

What's on the CD?

All assessments, tools, training instruments, and PowerPoint presentations included in this workbook are also available on the accompanying CD. Follow the instructions in the appendix, "Using the Compact Disc," at the back of the workbook or read "How to Use This CD.doc" on the CD.

Icons

For easy reference, icons are included in the margins throughout this workbook to help you quickly locate key elements in education design and instruction. Here are the icons and what they represent:

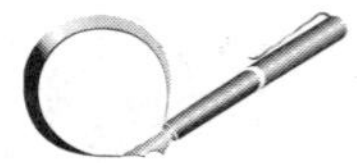

Assessment: Appears when an agenda or learning activity includes an assessment or evaluation.

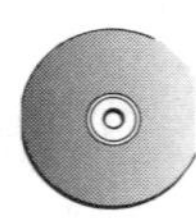

CD: Indicates materials included on the CD accompanying this workbook.

Clock: Indicates suggested timeframes for an activity.

Discussion Questions: Points out questions to use in exploring significant aspects of the training and in debriefing an activity.

Key Point: Alerts you to key points that you should emphasize to the participants or that are particularly salient for you as the facilitator.

Learning Activity: Indicates a structured exercise for use in a training session.

PowerPoint Slide: Indicates PowerPoint presentations and slides that you can use individually.

Tool: Identifies an item that offers information participants will find useful in the training session and on the job.

Training Instrument: Identifies participatory materials designed to enhance the learning experience for trainees.

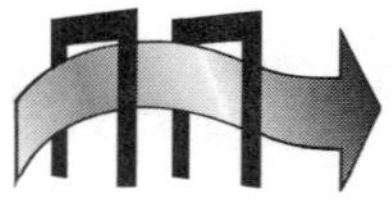

What to Do Next: Denotes recommendations for what to do after reading a particular section of the workbook.

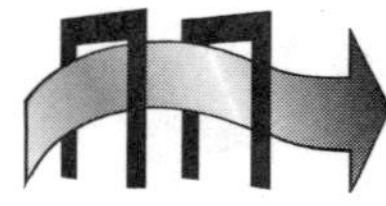

What to Do Next

- Study the contents of this workbook to learn for yourself what resources it contains.
- Review the contents of the CD and open a few of the items on it to be sure you know how to access them.

- Review the next chapter to learn about some of the challenges of diversity and potential pitfalls of diversity initiatives.
- Start constructing your own business case for diversity.

◆◆◆

Putting together a thorough diversity business case is necessary before you can seek funds for diversity development in an organization. Chapter 2 has been designed to assist you in this task. The chapter will also help you differentiate myth from fact in the diversity business case and help you avoid some of the most common pitfalls in diversity initiatives.

Chapter 2

Rewriting the Business Case for Diversity Development

What's In This Chapter?

- Summary of the challenges in the diversity field and some possible solutions
- Discussion of the potential pitfalls of diversity initiatives
- Analysis of the key issues commonly associated with

Nobody outside of a baby carriage or a judge's chamber believes in an unprejudiced point of view.

– Lillian Hellman (1905–1984), American playwright

You have spent weeks preparing for a meeting with the top leadership of your organization. Your objective is to establish a sound case for a diversity initiative. You know that you are about to face strong objections from key people. You also know that any diversity initiative needs firm commitment from the top, so this presentation is very important. You turn on your LCD projector, open your carefully designed PowerPoint presentation, and proudly say:

> Diversity is not a "feel-good" process. We are not here because we want to change the world. We are not here because "developing our diversity initiative is the right thing to do" either... even though we may all believe it is. We are here because diversity is a business imperative.

OK—good start. Then, before the next slide, one of the leaders says, "I understand it's important to protect the organization from lawsuits but, frankly, things seem to be fine without diversity initiatives. In fact, isn't it true that starting diversity programs may actually make the plant relations worse? Forgive the skepticism, but I don't see how this is a business imperative."

This chapter will help answer that remark. It will give you information on the following topics:

- the need for objectivity in diversity development
- ways to avoid making things worse
- directions for rewriting the diversity business case.

Understanding and Countering the Lack of Objectivity

Let's say a graduate student in zoology wants to find out whether the oxygen levels in the blood of bears can be improved when they eat more berries. She puts forth the following hypotheses:

1. Berries improve the blood oxygen levels of bears.
2. Berries do not improve the blood oxygen levels of bears.

Unless the student produces berries for a living or has a relative whose fame was made connecting berries and oxygen levels, it is unlikely the study results will deeply and personally affect her one way or another. It is fairly easy for her to be objective. Either berries help or they don't.

Conversely, however, the issue of discrimination does matter for most people. It touches a chord that is more than mere academic curiosity. Here are some possible reasons for the excessive subjectivity and lack of clear standards of practice that plague the diversity development field:

- Diversity trainers are the bear *and* the berry. They are not researchers who could not care less about what happens to either entity. They have felt the sting of being shunned for being black, white, Latino, women, men, old, young, lesbian, Muslim, overweight, disabled . . . take your pick. No one is neutral.
- Trainers are practitioners working with real people, not with laboratory experiments. They are often not trained in the rules of objective scientific research.
- Members of this profession are internal or external consultants with busy lives and hectic jobs. They often have little time to read com-

plicated social psychology and organizational development research reports.

- Diversity consultants, internal and external, come from a variety of professional backgrounds. There are no official standards to comply with or official competencies expected to be achieved. (There is considerable danger that such lack of standards may hurt clients and/or organizations.)
- There is a widespread perception that members of minority groups have more credibility or are more qualified to do diversity work than are members of majority groups, regardless of training or level of expertise.
- Diversity development practitioners, organizational development (OD) researchers, and social psychologists don't seem to talk to each other and thus fail to make the necessary connections that would benefit the diversity field.

So, what is the solution to this dilemma? How can one become better educated, short of obtaining a PhD in a field such as OD, social psychology, or international relations? Here are a few ideas:

- Regularly search through a scholarly database and locate actual research reports that may help you understand this complex issue.
- Make sure that diversity task forces and development groups include both majority and minority members—and listen to all voices. There are wisdom and learning in all comments. Nothing should be dismissed as silly rumblings of people who just "don't get it." Whenever people don't get it, there is probably a reason for that and it is important to know what that reason is.
- Play the devil's advocate. Take provocative positions. What if the findings are wrong? What if the plans don't work? Try hard to look at various angles and carefully analyze assumptions. At the very least, find out what the assumptions are and test them constantly.

Can Diversity Development Make Things Worse?

Aspiring doctors often learn that one of the primary rules in practicing medicine is never do harm to anyone. Maybe diversity practitioners should take heed of this advice.

In *Leadership and Self-Deception: Getting Out of the Box* (Arbinger Institute, 2000), a story is told of a Hungarian doctor who discovered to his dismay that he and other physicians were somehow contributing to the deaths of their patients. Dr. Ignaz Semmelweis, an obstetrician and medical educator at the Vienna Lying-in Hospital in the mid-1800s, was appalled at the death rates in the maternity ward under his responsibility. He was further concerned when he realized that the ward being run by midwives had a lower mortality rate than the ward run by doctors.

The reason for this peculiar state of affairs was the lack of understanding of germ science in 19th-century Austria. At that time, hospital doctors were also researchers, did work at the morgues, and considered it a matter of pride to present themselves with blood-stained clothes. When Semmelweis advocated and adopted the simple habit of hand washing, germ transmission dropped and the maternity death rates reached normal levels.

This story could be a metaphor for diversity training. Because diversity as a goal in itself has lately been such a truism in society, pitfalls of diversity initiatives may have been ignored. Just like the 19th-century Hungarian and Viennese doctors, it is possible for diversity practitioners to unwittingly do harm instead of good.

A few examples of possible "harm doing" caused by well-intentioned diversity initiatives include

- raising awareness of diversity-related problems without either the commitment or the resources to address their causes
- encouraging high-ranking employees to be "honest and open" during diversity discussions without previously informing them of possible legal dangers related to testimonies
- engendering a feeling of exclusion among employees who belong to the majority group because they feel that initiatives focused on minority groups will not benefit them
- including only members of minority groups on diversity committees
- generating myriad minority-specific initiatives that could reinforce the perception of differences among organizational members
- prompting fear and false harmony instead of trust and positive conflict resolution.

Another interesting metaphor for our work as diversity practitioners is the movie "Field of Dreams." In it, James Earl Jones' character advises Kevin Costner's character to build a special baseball field. "If you build it, they will come," Jones suggests in his deep-bass voice. "They" means every stakeholder imaginable: ghost players of the past, fans, baseball enthusiasts. Costner follows the advice and ultimately saves his farm—a beautiful happy ending. Perhaps the diversity field has adopted a "Field of Dreams" mentality. If we build a diversity initiative, it will all be OK. If training is done, everyone will feel better. If diverse employees are hired, productivity will automatically rise.

Unfortunately, a business is not a Hollywood set. There are plenty of pitfalls. Poor and damaging training can be delivered and, despite practitioners' best intentions, a diversity field of dreams will not instantaneously be populated by new, prejudice-free players and fans.

Von Bergen, Soper, and Foster (2002) have suggested various diversity education mistakes that cause initiatives to go awry. These mistakes include

- trainer biases and personal agendas
- selection of trainers based on their advocacy for certain groups
- brief training sessions responding to crisis situations
- training framed as remediation rather than advancement
- language that does not clearly distinguish the diversity initiative from old Affirmative Action practices
- excessively narrow focus presented in a way that excludes certain groups and relevant topics from the discussion.

Training professionals must realize their power to influence and their status as non-neutral observers. They are part of and have an impact on the culture they are attempting to change. Without these realizations, *yes, diversity training can make matters worse.*

Rewriting the Business Case for Diversity Initiatives

Traditionally, the business case for developing diversity initiatives has been built on the following five premises:

1. The demographics of the United States are changing. There are more women and people of color in the workplace then ever before, and their numbers are increasing.

2. Today's economy is global and interdependent. Even small businesses may need to have productive contact with people from all over the world.

3. Even if a particular business doesn't yet employ many people of different cultures and/or ethnicities, and even if it does not do business internationally, it will probably want to market to an increasingly diverse internal market. An all-white, all-male workforce may make a company vulnerable to marketing blunders and thereby affect the organization's image in the community.

4. Heterogeneous groups are more productive because of the diversity of ideas and perspectives that members of minority groups bring to the table.

5. Societal pressures and antidiscrimination legislation make it particularly dangerous for organizations not to invest in diversity relations. Lawsuits are costly from all angles: branding, community image, and even the value of stock.

To rewrite the business case for diversity initiatives we need to discuss all of those premises.

CHANGING DEMOGRAPHICS

This is probably the simplest and most compelling reason for a diversity initiative in any organization. A visit to the U.S. Census Bureau Website will provide the following information:

- Almost 18 percent of the U.S. population speaks a language other than English at home.

- In 1970, 83 percent of the population was Caucasian. By 2002 the Caucasian population share had dropped to 69 percent. Census projections indicate that, by 2050, this percentage will drop further to 53 percent. Considering that roughly 50 percent of the population is male and 50 percent female, it may be concluded that the white male population is a minority *today.*

- Between 1995 and 2050 the American population will increase unequally, as follows:
  - white, non-Hispanic people, 7.4 percent
  - people of Hispanic origin, 258.3 percent
  - black, non-Hispanic people, 69.5 percent
  - American Indians, 83.0 percent
  - Asian and Pacific Islanders, 269.1 percent.

It is thus not difficult to see the changing trend of the majority–minority composition of the U.S. population. For instance, Caucasian Americans under 18 years of age are projected to be a minority among other Americans of the same age by 2030. It is reasonable to assume that such a trend will sooner or later affect the workplace and require that HR practitioners develop appropriate interventions. Furthermore, large cities and certain U.S. states already face such demographic changes on a large scale.

GLOBAL ECONOMY

In *The Future of Corporate Globalization: From the Extended Order to the Global Village,* Jeremiah Sullivan (2002) has distinguished two aspects of globalization. The first one, characterized by an expansion of trade and investment across borders, is not new. It has been expanding steadily throughout the 19th and 20th centuries. The second aspect, which Sullivan labels globalization "linkages," has to do with the increased interdependence among nations, and the impact of one nation's economic and political woes on another.

Unlike standard global commerce, globalization linkages are a more recent phenomenon. A symptom of a highly interlinked global economy can be found in the impact of the recent Asian and the Mexican economic crises on the U.S. economy. In simple terms, what happens across the world can come back to haunt U.S. organizations.

DIVERSE MARKETING, CORPORATE IMAGE, AND MARKETING BLUNDERS

The need for organizations to understand the cultural practices of each group within their markets often justifies diversity development programs. The rationale is that minority group representation within organizations may prevent serious marketing blunders. Diversity development programs could help sensitize company executives and recruiters to the need for a diverse employee workforce.

That argument is not baseless. For instance, here are a few examples of U.S. marketing and service blunders experienced by Brazilians:

- U.S. companies frequently send Spanish-language marketing materials, labels, contracts, and other business items to Brazil. Because the language spoken in Brazil is Portuguese rather than Spanish, Brazilians are often surprised and offended.
- U.S. publishing houses send hundreds of American titles to Brazil, hoping the local literary agents will find homes for them. But the subject matter is often of no relevance to local readers, concerning instead topics of limited international interest or applicability.
- It is common for U.S. executives to arrive in Brazil with multiple meetings set up back to back in order to make the best use of their time. Typically, however, meetings take longer in a country where relationship building is vital for business success.

The problem with the marketing argument as a basis for diversity initiatives is that the presence of minority employees within an organization doesn't necessarily prevent cultural faux pas. For instance, not all U.S. Americans of Hispanic descent are familiar with the cultural rules of their heritage, and it is perfectly possible that a Caucasian employee will bring valuable international marketing experiences to the table.

Although it is true that culturally diverse employees may be able to share invaluable experiences, the key is to avoid pigeonholing anyone within specific areas as a result of his or her cultural heritage. Such practice is career-limiting, myopic, and discriminatory. We do, however, highly recommend that you take multiculturalism into consideration as you plan all marketing *and* professional development initiatives.

INCREASED PRODUCTIVITY OF HETEROGENEOUS GROUPS

Are heterogeneous groups really more productive? Not necessarily, but as is true of other diversity-related assumptions, the following assumption is repeated so often that people seldom bother to dispute it: Diversity is important because diverse teams produce better and more creative results. Good teams include males and females; people from all walks of life; people from various departments; homosexuals, bisexuals, and heterosexuals; people of various personality styles, ages, tenure levels, and educational backgrounds. And, of course, lest we forget—good teams have blacks, whites, Asians, Latinos, Native Americans, and a few foreigners. Just bring all people together and, Bingo! innovative products are ready to ship to Timbuktu with a perfect marketing campaign and packaging that is likely to please people from all over.

Sure. There is just one bothersome little detail to consider: Numerous studies have been conducted trying to demonstrate this very point—and they have failed. To date, study results on the impact of demographic diversity on productivity are at best contradictory, and diversity is frequently referred to as a "double-edged sword" (see Cox, 2001).

There is some evidence that diversity in perspectives and diversity in functionality (the kind of diversity that is generated by representatives of different functions and departments) improve the quality of the solutions reached by teams. If it is assumed that cultural differences are accompanied by differences in perspectives, culturally heterogeneous teams may indeed be desirable.

Cultural differences, however, are not necessarily accompanied by differences in perspectives, ideas, or thought processes. Culture indicates a tendency rather than a prescription toward some specific behavior. Within the same culture, individuals vary greatly.

Moreover, individuals with culturally diverse backgrounds who are perceived as a "better fit" with the *organizational* culture are more likely to be hired and rewarded. As a result, a seemingly culturally and racially heterogeneous team could be a team of similar perspectives and thought processes wrapped in a multicolored and multicultural package.

The productivity argument is, therefore, partly false and partly true. It is false because diverse teams are not automatically more productive, and sometimes they appear to be more diverse than they really are. The argument is true, on the other hand, because diverse teams *are* likely to experience more conflict and diversity education may offer team members exactly the support they need to increase their effectiveness and job satisfaction.

SOCIAL PRESSURES AND DISCRIMINATION LEGISLATION

A November 1996 story in *The New York Times* included the transcripts of a secretly taped conversation between senior executives at Texaco Corporation—the treasurer, senior coordinator for personnel services, and senior assistant treasurer. One of the participants referred to Texaco's black employees as "black jelly beans" and observed that "all black jelly beans agree." The other replied that "all black jelly beans seemed to be glued to the bottom." Two days later, Texaco's stock fell vertiginously and there were calls for a national boycott of Texaco products. Later that year, Texaco agreed to pay more than $140 million to resolve a federal lawsuit brought by minority employees (Eichenwald, 1996).

Stories like that are often told in support of the "legal" argument for diversity. Organizations commonly want to "check the diversity box" by having *some* program that shows *some* judge *some*day that they did try to improve relations *some*what.

So how real is the legal argument? It's mostly real. It is true that the number of discrimination lawsuits has greatly increased in recent years. Also increased are employees' chances of winning their cases . . . and punitive damages. According to Jury Verdict Research, a legal research firm quoted in an article by Grensing-Pophal (2001), an employee's chances of winning increased from 45 percent in 1994 to 72 percent in 1999. Moreover, the average compensatory award went from $128,000 in 1996 to $221,612 in 1999. During the 1990s the number of discrimination lawsuits against corporations more than tripled.

What is the role of diversity initiatives in this environment? *Protection.* A New Jersey attorney cited in an article by Prince (2003) argued that training can reduce liability and damages. To support the claim, a U.S. Supreme Court ruling was cited stating that punitive damages are not, in general, awarded against companies that take reasonable steps to train managers in discrimination prevention.

Why then is the argument partly false? Because having a one-hour video on valuing diversity is unlikely to do much good—and it could very easily do harm. Employees might interpret that the company's approach to diversity is of the "diversity-checkbox" variety—the company provides just enough to be able to put a checkmark in the "supplied diversity training" column of some official form. Instead of improving diversity relations, such training might cause resentment and anger. Moreover, employees' lawyers could argue that such activities were merely a ploy to protect the organization and a cover-up for real diversity-related problems.

Also, diversity initiatives are not exempt from legal hazards of their own. Remember the discussion of whether diversity practitioners can do harm? Here are two common legal diversity traps:

1. **Confidentiality:** How many times have you been asked to "be open and honest" during a diversity training event? Marshall Lachmann, an attorney based in Dayton, Ohio, has explained that client–counsel confidentiality protection applies to attorneys and their clients *only*—certainly not to diversity trainers and participants in training sessions. It also doesn't apply to diversity consultants running cultural audits, unless they are licensed attorneys operating as the organization's counsel. If managers decide to be "honest" during a session and they make discriminatory remarks, those remarks could be used against them and the organization (Delikat, 1995).

   Logical conclusion: Continue asking for confidentiality but understand the limitations of the request. Make sure that managers understand the legal risks involved in being too open during a diversity session. If openness is really required, try one-on-one coaching instead. Finally, have an attorney coordinate all phases and aspects of a diversity cultural audit. Whatever is uncovered through such an audit may be subpoenaed later.

2. **Topics Included:** If the company's curriculum for diversity is too narrow, certain groups could use this against the organization in later litigation. For instance, someone could say that "this organization pays such little attention to *our* group that it was the only group not mentioned during our diversity initiative (Segal, 1995).

In conclusion, the legal argument for diversity development is very real, but so are the legal dangers attached to diversity development initiatives. Make sure that you tread carefully on this dangerous legal ground. Involve the organization's legal counsel in all diversity relations processes, including the ones pursued as a result of reading this book. If you are an external consultant and not a lawyer, clearly let your clients know what you can and cannot do for them.

What to Do Next

- Develop your own diversity business case to explain why you are considering a diversity initiative.
- Start thinking about how you will measure the success of your initiative. Identify what you are trying to improve and how progress toward improvement can be measured.

◆◆◆

In the chapters that follow you will read about the most likely causes for diversity conflicts and learn how to channel diversity development toward team effectiveness and performance improvement *while doing the least possible harm*. Chapter 3 summarizes research conducted on the fields of psychology and organizational development. Because this research is highly relevant to the practice of diversity development and provides a rationale for all exercises contained in this book, we strongly suggest that you read it thoroughly. Additionally, consult the sources provided in the For Further Reading section and familiarize yourself with research on the origins of prejudice, social discrimination, diverse team effectiveness, and similarity bias.

Chapter 3

What Does Science Tell Us About Diversity?

What's in This Chapter?

- Discussion of the limitations inherent in diversity research
- Definitions of key diversity-related terminology
- Review of the psychological and social bases for prejudice and discrimination

The most terrible atrocities committed by humans have often not been the acts of criminals or madmen, but of ordinary, loyal citizens acting in the presumed interests of their group against another group.
–John Duckitt, *The Social Psychology of Prejudice,* 1994

The information contained in this chapter is particularly relevant for diversity development practitioners. It is the basis for the Conversity philosophy explained earlier and is vitally linked to the diversity competencies presented in chapter 4.

Because the scope of this workbook doesn't allow for a more detailed analysis of a very complex topic, the reader is directed to the sources contained in the For Further Reading section at the back of this book. In particular, a detailed literature search report is available in a white paper titled "Research Connections in Diversity Development" (Wildermuth, 2004).

Research Limitations

If you decide to do background research on diversity, you should approach every text, every study, every book—including this one—with a healthy dose of skepticism and scientific curiosity. There are no clear-cut answers in diver-

sity relations. Keep the following points in mind as you search through diversity literature:

- Prejudice is a complex phenomenon. People could be prejudiced against a certain minority group and not against another. Prejudice against a group cannot be generalized to other groups.
- Legal and social constraints prevent many organizations from releasing sensitive data, so available information may be incomplete and unreliable.
- When research is conducted in a "laboratory" setting (that is, in a controlled setting that attempts to simulate aspects of the workplace environment), it is impossible to completely reproduce the complexities of the real workplace. It is, therefore, tricky to generalize the findings.
- When research is conducted in a "field" setting (that is, the workplace), it is practically impossible to completely isolate all factors that may affect the findings. For instance, higher employee satisfaction could result from the good work of a new leader rather than a diversity development intervention.
- *Correlation* doesn't mean *cause*. Even if high turnover correlates with increased ethnic diversity within a team, that doesn't mean that the diversity necessarily caused the turnover. Likewise, if participation in a certain diversity education system correlates with higher productivity, it may still not be possible to say that the training caused the increase in productivity.
- Make sure the data reviewed are current and reflect the current social atmosphere (for example, a 1950s-era study on diversity may not have relevance today).

Key Definitions

Diversity development requires a basic understanding of key terms in diversity. What follows is a brief discussion of each of these terms.

ATTITUDES

Attitudes are one's innermost thoughts, feelings, and general tendencies. Although attitudes are not *necessarily* translated into behaviors, they often are acted out, even when such translation occurs in a subtle and unintentional way.

Table 3–1
Definitions of Key Terms Addressed in This Chapter

Attitudes	A person's innermost thoughts, feelings, and general tendencies
Prejudice	A negative attitude toward a person resulting from that person's membership in a certain group
Stereotype	A perceived group trait (true or false) assigned to individuals belonging to that group
Stereotype rigidity	Resistance to the disproving of a stereotype despite considerable contradictory evidence
Discrimination	A pattern of behaviors that isolate and victimize members of certain groups because of their membership in those groups
Racism	A race-specific form of discrimination, affecting only members of certain racial groups or those perceived to be members of those groups.
Symbolic racism	A covert, subtle form of modern racism that is often an unintended by-product of unconscious prejudices. Behaviors associated with symbolic racism include differences in body language, unwillingness to engage in voluntary social interactions, and others.

It is important to differentiate this definition of *attitude* from its colloquial use. For instance, if people say, "Jane has an attitude," they probably mean that Jane presents herself in a negative and nay-sayer way. If, however, you read somewhere in this book "it is important to take into consideration Jane's attitudes," the meaning is "you need to consider Jane's thoughts, feelings, and general inclinations toward this issue."

PREJUDICE

Literally, *prejudice* means to prejudge. Everyone prejudges situations daily. Deciding whether to cross a street is based on the prejudged probability of being run over by a car. Hiring is only possible if HR professionals are able to prejudge a candidate's potential for success within a certain organization.

The definition of *prejudice* used here, however, is the positive or negative prejudgment of a person based on this person's membership in a certain group.

STEREOTYPES

To *stereotype* is to attribute to an *individual* the characteristics *perceived* as pertaining to his or her group. The word *perception* is key to this definition because the group characteristics attributed to this individual may or may not be "real." In fact, in diversity relations, perception tends to matter far more than reality.

The origins of the word are commonly attributed to the early days of the press when text was composed through the juxtaposition of various metal pieces (one for each letter). Because the title of the newspaper was always the same, it was cast into a single metal piece, called a *stereotype.*

Stereotyping is a normal human reaction. Humans infer new information from old experiences. For example, if a person has had a bad experience with several members of a certain group, it is not unreasonable for this person to be leery in his or her next contact with another member of the same group.

Arguably, therefore, the problem is not so much in the stereotype itself as it is in *stereotype rigidity.* This is defined as the inability or unwillingness to disprove a certain stereotype even in the presence of abundant contradictory evidence.

DISCRIMINATION AND RACISM

Prejudice is an attitude—thoughts and feelings that may or may not materialize in actions. *Discrimination,* on the other hand, is a pattern of *behaviors* that victimize individuals because of their membership in a certain group. Discrimination brings to real life what human beings have inside their heads.

Racism can be defined as a race-specific genre of discrimination. People *perceived* as belonging to a certain race are discriminated against overtly or subtly.

The word *perception* is again key to this definition. Because genetic differences between the so-called human races are arguably small, the important parameter is not the biology of racism, but its psychological and anthropological interpretations. In other words, what matters is not whether two people are truly biologically different, but whether each of them perceives the other as *different* or as *similar*. If differences are perceived, it is also important to consider *how significant* these differences are perceived to be. For example, two friends may easily perceive that they have different facial features. If, however, these physical differences are *perceived* by the two friends as irrelevant, such differences are unlikely to change the friends' relationship.

Another key element to understanding racism is the presence of "symbolic" or "covert" racism. Modern forms of racism are typically much less obvious than those exhibited during the civil-rights struggles in the 1960s in most of the United States. Modern racism can be demonstrated through body language, tone of voice, willingness to be near the person, and other subtle behaviors (see Knuckey and D'Andra Orey, 2000). It is also more likely to be expressed in informal and voluntary situations, such as employee networks, friendships, happy hours, and other social gatherings outside of work.

Why do diversity practitioners need to know about symbolic racism?

- The very subtlety of symbolic racism makes it practically impossible for organizations to develop and enforce policies against it. Symbolic racism, therefore, may only be reduced through long-term education interventions at the *attitude* level. Organizations, however, are often reluctant to address employee attitudes during mandatory training sessions.
- Symbolic racism may explain why minority and majority members of organizations often perceive the presence of racism differently. If racism is subtle it can be easily denied by those who do not experience it firsthand.
- Even the best-intentioned majority group members are likely to exhibit some level of symbolic racism. The history of severe racism in U.S. society is too recent for it not to have left its mark.
- Informal employee relationships have an impact on a person's ability to be successful at an organization. Mentoring and information sharing often take place in voluntary social connections and events. People excluded from these events are at a disadvantage.

Psychological and Social Foundations of Prejudice

How relevant is prejudice in the workplace? Some people may argue that prejudice is unimportant because it is not directly connected to *behaviors*. Others argue that prejudice and discrimination are interconnected and should both be addressed in diversity interventions.

The authors take the second view. Because modern discrimination is often subtle it is almost impossible to reduce it without interventions at the attitudinal level. Practitioners who attempt to affect both prejudice and discrimination, however, need to understand where prejudiced attitudes come from.

Three topics provide a valuable background for diversity development: social identity bias and categorization, similarity bias, and intercultural development stages.

SOCIAL IDENTITY BIAS AND CATEGORIZATION

Social identity bias is a collection of positive attitudes people tend to exhibit toward members of their own group. Human beings tend to form groups and to prefer members of their group over others. The process of forming groups or categories is also commonly referred to by social psychologists as *categorization.*

Because social identity bias and categorization are strong human tendencies, practitioners are wise to work *with them* rather than against them. It is reasonable to assume that any training that goes with—rather than against—normal human tendencies is more likely to "stick." For instance, one objective for diversity development may be to encourage diverse employees to perceive themselves as members of the same group. This perception is likely to affect the way they see and relate to one another.

SIMILARITY BIAS

It is common for diversity training sessions to be titled "Valuing Differences" or "Celebrating Diversity." The problem is that most human beings do not value differences at all; they value similarities instead. Similarity bias—a collection of positive attitudes exhibited by most humans toward people perceived to be the same as they—is another powerful human tendency and one that can be channeled successfully through diversity development sessions. Why? Because *perception* again is key. If training affects people's ability to perceive one another as the same rather than as different, similarity bias is likely to kick in automatically.

INTERCULTURAL DEVELOPMENT STAGES

Milton Bennett (1993), a leading interculturalist, created a model for intercultural development that is highly relevant to diversity relations practice.

According to Bennett's model, people progress in a series of stages, ranging between ethnocentrism (the belief that a person's cultural norms are universally accepted) to ethnorelativism (a state of true multiculturalism in which people are able to accept cultural differences and live comfortably within a culturally diverse society). His model helps practitioners decide on the proper intervention for a group, based on the group's level of intercultural development. For example, if a group's view of differences is highly negative, a "celebrating differences" program is likely to cause more harm than good by prompting members to become even more prejudiced. A process emphasizing similarities among all human beings is more likely to be successful.

So What?

It is not only nice to know how prejudices are formed, how diverse groups interact, and how humans progress through various levels of intercultural development. That information is essential for the serious diversity development practitioner. It is the basis for the Conversity philosophy introduced in this book. Indeed, why Conversity rather than diversity? If humans perceive themselves as similar to one another and as members of the same group, they are far more likely to tolerate one another's differences. Moreover, Bennett's study shows that a focus on differences may lead a prejudiced person toward an even more prejudiced state. It makes sense, therefore, to focus on similarities first and include discussions on the value of differences second.

What to Do Next

- Explore the For Further Reading section at the back of this book for additional resource materials on the social psychology of prejudice. We highly recommend Duckitt's (1994) comprehensive view of the topic.
- Complete a diversity awareness inventory to better understand your own hidden biases (see Assessment 13–1: Diversity Self-Awareness).
- Participate in a diversity development session or take a college course on the topic to increase your own self-awareness and enable you to discuss the topic with others.

◆◆◆

The following chapter continues the exploration of diversity development, specifically addressing diversity and return-on-investment, designing an effective development program, and identifying diversity competencies.

Chapter 4

Evaluating and Planning Diversity Training: What Works?

What's in This Chapter?

- Discussion of the challenges inherent in diversity evaluation
- Description of the key characteristics of an effective diversity initiative
- Summary of the key competencies addressed by the training modules included in this book
- Review of the conditions associated with true multiculturalism in organizations

Never try to reason the prejudice out of a man. It was not reasoned into him, and cannot be reasoned out.

– Sidney Smith (1771–1845), English clergyman

As described in chapter 3, diversity is a complex and multidisciplinary field. This very complexity makes a return-on-investment (ROI) study on diversity initiatives particularly tricky. Of course, progress may be tracked and measures determined to guide the way. Your department is unlikely to continue receiving funding for training initiatives if movement in the right direction is not demonstrated.

This chapter will offer evaluation tips, provide a sample Level 1 evaluation survey, discuss what makes effective and ineffective programs, offer a list of diversity competencies to consider in your planning, and end with a vision of the multicultural organization that is more likely to result in success.

Diversity Program Evaluation

A common problem for facilitators is receiving feedback on a program only *after* it is completed. Although participant feedback certainly is invaluable for future improvements, it is preferable to start using the feedback immediately to help the current group. Sometimes minor issues such as table arrangements, sound, heating, and absence of refreshments may affect the success of a program. You want to hear about those problems *as they occur,* not at the end of the day.

To encourage immediate participant feedback, create an Evaluation Parking Lot with flipchart paper and pads of sticky notes. Tell participants to post feedback in the parking lot at any time. Ideally, participants should feel comfortable using the parking lot and should let you know of any small distractions or improvement suggestions. Make sure you check the parking lot frequently for new postings.

Levels of Evaluation for Training Programs

In 1959, Dr. Donald Kirkpatrick defined four levels of evaluation to use when measuring the outcome of training programs:

Level 1: Did you like the program?

Level 2: Did you learn from it?

Level 3: Are you applying what you learned at work?

Level 4: Did the training program produce a bottom-line effect?

Included on the accompanying CD-ROM is a Sample Level 1 Evaluation (Assessment 13–2), which you may distribute to participants at the end of each module. You may notice that the sample does not include the traditional Likert scales so often adopted in training. Here is the rationale for this choice: If participants are given the option to simply check a box, they will do only that. Facilitators, however, often find it much more useful to receive a specific comment than to know that on a scale of 1 to 5, the program was a 4.

Of course, one of the problems of a qualitative survey such as Assessment 13–2 is that it is harder to track and quantify. Depending on the size of your groups you may need to use a more traditional multiple-choice questionnaire and encourage participants to add written comments.

Here are some possible ways to encourage more comprehensive responses:

- Offer small prizes to participants who add written comments to the evaluations.
- Give participants enough time at the end of the session to complete the evaluation and leave on time.

Of course, a Level 1 evaluation survey is only a small portion of your evaluation. A common criticism of diversity initiatives is precisely that although participants may enjoy them, long-term benefits are hard to quantify. There is no easy solution to this problem. Accurately measuring the ROI for diversity development could be a costly and cumbersome proposition for organizations. It is a good idea to keep in mind that a definitive answer is unlikely. Too many factors, after all, affect diversity relations, including leadership, external environment, internal culture, reward systems, recruitment, time, and so forth. For instance, even if you discover that turnover was reduced by 10 percent after your training intervention, such reduction may or may not be the result of the training itself.

Consider the following tips as you plan the process:

- Decide beforehand (when designing your training program) what measurements you will choose to focus on. Possible options include turnover, productivity, sales, number of EEOC (Equal Employment Opportunity Commission) issues, number of client complaints, and client satisfaction results.
- Expect no miracles. It is useless, for example, to plan a one-time, one-hour diversity session and attempt to find out whether the program generated a significant productivity increase. It won't.
- Seek legal advice before implementing any survey or data collection process. It is possible that results of such surveys could be subpoenaed in any subsequent litigation.
- Decide how you will isolate the various factors affecting the results you are tracking. Time, for instance, is a key factor that influences teams and it's very tricky to isolate. Because team longevity tends to improve its performance, after a certain period of time any team is likely to work better, with or without your training intervention.
- Any kind of training intervention could positively or negatively affect group processes. This includes training conducted for members of other groups (leaders, support personnel, administration, customer service, and so forth) whose work has an impact on the group you are analyzing. Not only diversity training affects diversity relations.
- Beware of researcher biases. Often the same person, organization, or unit runs the training needs analysis, the training itself, and the train-

ing evaluation that follows it. Under such conditions biases creep in, regardless of one's best intentions.

As you plan the evaluation processes consider how much time and effort should reasonably be spent. Not everything can or should be measured. Evaluation costs should be proportionate to the costs of the program designed and the problem you are attempting to solve.

Because a full-blown ROI study is often costly and time-consuming, it may be useful to consider alternative terminology: return-on-expectations (ROE). What were the initial goals? What was expected to happen as a result of the interventions? What did participants themselves expect? Whatever that was, did it happen?

Finally, always rely on multiple sources of data. For example, many organizations rely on employee satisfaction surveys as a measure of success. Such surveys, however, may have limited value when studied in isolation. The first problem with satisfaction surveys is that they typically confuse comfort and effectiveness. Two people could be highly comfortable together: they might enjoy the same hobbies, share similar communication and learning styles, and agree on myriad other issues. Because of their many commonalities, similarity bias would kick in and these two individuals would likely report very favorably on one another.

Effectiveness, however, is likely to depend on factors such as

- ability to divide roles for maximum effectiveness
- willingness to hold team members accountable for team goals
- willingness to engage in task-related conflict when needed for the good of the team.

Excessive similarity (as in similar styles, perspectives, and preferred team roles) is very likely to breed comfort but may not lead to effectiveness.

A second problem with satisfaction surveys is that satisfaction and productivity do not necessarily walk hand in hand. A group severely plagued by groupthink (the tendency to make group harmony and unanimity the first priority, at all costs) could also be highly satisfied—in fact, a state of near-euphoria commonly characterizes such groups and prevents them from reaching high-quality decisions.

Effective Diversity Programs

If results of your diversity interventions are not as expected, the conclusion need not be that diversity training doesn't work. An alternative explanation may be that there is a flaw in the program's design.

Effective diversity processes often are

- **long-term:** diversity relations are seldom affected by a single workshop, no matter how well received it is. Reinforcement is key to success.
- **customized to participants' needs:** specific community needs and participants' current levels of intercultural and team development need to be taken into consideration. The same intervention that would work wonders with a more sophisticated group could backfire with a less experienced one.
- **experiential:** designs incorporating role plays and other exercises that lead to greater empathy are more likely to have a long-term impact.
- **comprehensive:** team success is related to myriad skill areas, such as conflict resolution, communications, and feedback. Each of those interventions will need to be long-term, customized, and constantly reinforced. Knowledge, skill building, and attitude development competencies ought to be considered.

That last bullet point includes a rather controversial recommendation: the inclusion of attitude development in the diversity curriculum. Many oppose this view, arguing that it is unrealistic and inappropriate to run attitudinal interventions in the workplace.

Indeed it is true that a change of attitudes requires a lengthy process, is self-motivated, and cannot be imposed by an organization. There are significant challenges from both legal and developmental standpoints in any attitudinal training. Here, however, are two considerations for targeting attitude change during comprehensive diversity initiatives:

1. **Attitudes and behaviors commonly travel together.** Attitudes and behaviors tend to affect one another in a never-ending cycle. Addressing only one of the two could be like building a table on two legs. Moreover, as discussed in chapter 3, modern discrimination is often

subtle. Examples include greater-than-normal person-to-person distance; a harsher tone of voice; unwillingness to befriend, help, or invite to informal networks; and other covert but hurtful behaviors. Behavioral training and company policies alone are unlikely to solve this problem.

2. **Prejudice may be unconscious.** Unfortunately, many expressions of discrimination are products of the unconscious prejudices and deeply ingrained biases many people don't know they have. Prejudice itself is not a behavior but a tendency toward a behavior, in the absence of social and legal constraints. Unless people become aware of such tendencies, they are unlikely to control them.

Another controversial issue in the attitudinal versus behavioral training debate is the inclusion of *values* in the training curriculum. A number of diversity practitioners shy away from any values discussions during diversity interventions. Values, however, are a highly relevant topic and one that needs not be taboo. Here are two reasons for including values:

1. **Organizations are value driven.** Many organizations include their values in mission and vision statements and consider an applicant's potential to share those values during selection processes.
2. **Value discussions cause significant conflict.** Value disputes between groups—especially when the discussions involve religious or moral values—are often a particularly serious problem at work.

This does not mean that diversity facilitators should try to change the expressed values of employees. Such attempt would indeed place the organization on dangerous moral and legal ground. We recommend that employees be given the skills needed to handle value disputes respectfully and appropriately.

One word of caution: Values and attitudes are sensitive topics. They should be handled professionally, respectfully, and only when participants are ready to address them. We recommend that values and prejudices *not* be addressed in the first workshop and that sufficient time be allotted for such discussions in subsequent sessions.

Diversity Competencies

Because diversity relations are affected by myriad factors, the complete list of diversity-related competencies is daunting. It would be impossible to address every competency in any single training event. A summarized competency list is given in this chapter to help diversity practitioners plan a road map for the training interventions they select from this book. Only competencies related to the training modules included in this book are listed here. A more detailed competency list is available in a white paper titled "Diversity Development Competencies at Individual, Team, and Leadership Levels" (Wildermuth and Gray, 2004).

The competencies listed here are divided according to the training module related to them and further identified as knowledge (K), attitude development (ATT), or skill (S).

MODULE 1 COMPETENCIES (CHAPTER 8: OUT OF THE BOX)

- Able to describe the impact of categorization on human relations (K)
- Able to describe the impact of categorization on informal professional networks and professional success (K)
- Able to use Conversity techniques to actively seek common ground with members of other groups (S)

MODULE 2 COMPETENCIES (CHAPTER 9: CULTURES AMD VALUES)

- Able to describe human cultures and their impact on human assumptions, values, beliefs, rituals, and behaviors (K)
- Willing to examine one's own cultural assumptions, values, beliefs, rituals, and behaviors (ATT)
- Willing to openly explore alternative cultural systems and their inherent logic (ATT)
- Able to choose nonjudgmental language when addressing cultural issues (S)

MODULE 3 COMPETENCIES (CHAPTER 10: FIRST IMPRESSIONS)

- Able to explain the origin of stereotypes and their impact on decision making (K)

- Awareness of one's own stereotypes and their origins (ATT)
- Willing to question assumptions and stereotypes for out-group members (ATT)
- Able to discard old stereotypes when new, disproving information is available (S)

MODULE 4 COMPETENCIES (CHAPTER 11: WALKING IN THEIR SHOES)

- Willing to explore and gain awareness of personal prejudices and connect them to life experiences and teachings (ATT, S)
- Able to explain the relationship between discrimination and prejudice (K)
- Able to describe subtle discriminatory behaviors involving body language, tone of voice, physical distance, and so forth (K)
- Able to recognize negative bias even when subtly expressed (S)

Toward a Multicultural Organization

Under the melting-pot ideal Americans should combine all cultures, values, and beliefs; mix them up over the fire of patriotism; and presto! Behold the American dream, a rehomogenized society reinvented from all its parts. But there is a problem with a melting pot: Its contents are tasteless. It reminds one of a thick vegetable soup in which distinct flavors are impossible to determine, except perhaps for one or two key flavors that tend to dominate.

The melting pot metaphor has been replaced by a salad bowl in which individual tastes and textures are preserved. But somehow the salad bowl seems limited, too. The lettuce doesn't learn from the tomato. The parts are still disconnected. The flavors do not seem to mix. A big part of the flavor is brought by the seasoning, which comes from outside rather than within.

A truly multicultural organization is a constantly evolving set of flavors. Unlike the melting pot, each component retains texture and individuality. Unlike the salad, they influence and change one another. When different cultures come into frequent contact they stretch toward one another—learn from each other.

The learning-and-effectiveness paradigm presented by Thomas and Ely (1996) predicted such stretch. Interestingly, learning-and-effectiveness organizations do not expect only minority groups to do the learning. When stretching occurs, it occurs throughout the organization. The community constantly reinvents itself as it absorbs the best that each group has to offer. Thomas and Ely suggested that the following eight preconditions are needed for a shift toward the learning-and-effectiveness paradigm:

1. The leadership must truly value differences in perspective.
2. The leadership must recognize that they are in it for the long haul.
3. The organization must never waver from the absolute requirement of high standards from all its members.
4. The organizational culture should foster personal development.
5. Openness should always be encouraged and rewarded.
6. Employees should feel valued and important to the success of an organization.
7. A clearly articulated mission must be the key guide for goal development.
8. The structure of the organization must be relatively egalitarian and nonbureaucratic.

Considering the research we conducted for this book, we add the following four conditions:

1. The organizational culture should foster creativity and positive conflict resolution. These are the most frequently found by-products of diversity and they must be encouraged if diverse organizations are to reap their highest rewards.
2. Organizational rewards should mostly be attached to teams rather than to individuals. Competition increases discrimination between groups and could increase negative by-products of diversity, such as relationship conflict.
3. Demographic diversity should be present at all levels of the organization. Contact among groups only reduces discrimination when it takes place among individuals of equal status. Otherwise, contact

could increase discrimination. Employees are more likely to pay attention to the environment around them than to organizational protestations of equality.

4. Conversity, the tireless search for common ground, should be a staple in all organizational and team endeavors. Conversity does not eliminate or trivialize differences. It simply opens the doors and enables people to learn from the differences. The search for common ground and the Thomas and Ely's learning-and-effectiveness paradigm should be present at all levels of the organization; be part of its mission and vision; and prominently appear in every marketing piece, every training program, and every major communication.

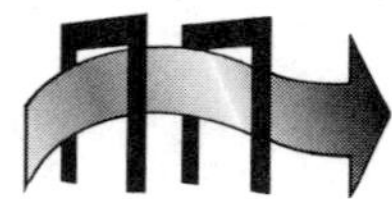

What to Do Next

- Have a preliminary consultation with your organization's legal counsel to discuss the diversity initiative.
- Decide whether and how to run a cultural audit. Remember to include multiple sources of information.
- Choose evaluation criteria and methodology. Take steps to reduce researcher bias.
- Briefly examine the learning modules included in this book (chapters 8 through 11) to familiarize yourself with the suggested contents of your first diversity training programs.

◆◆◆

Diversity initiatives may be carefully planned and still fail because of facilitation and methodology problems. The following chapter will help you further plan your diversity training intervention. It includes a discussion of effective facilitation and will connect the field of appreciative inquiry to diversity training.

Chapter 5

Facilitating Your Diversity Program

What's in This Chapter?

- Discussion of factors to be considered when selecting diversity facilitators
- Do's and don'ts when planning and preparing for diversity instruction
- Discussion of potential legal pitfalls in diversity development programs
- Review of the connections between diversity development and the appreciative inquiry field

The test of a first-rate intelligence is the ability to hold two opposed ideas in the mind at the same time, and still retain the ability to function.

– F. Scott Fitzgerald (1896–1940), American writer

Adding to the material presented in chapter 4, this chapter will give you more tips for creating and implementing an effective diversity development process, including information on facilitator selection, planning do's and don'ts, legal pitfalls, group arrangement, and room setup. A discussion of appreciative inquiry and diversity is included to help you frame your initiatives in a positive light.

Selection of Facilitators

Here is the good news: Diversity facilitators don't need to be either perfect or neutral. They are not necessarily diversity experts and would be wise to introduce themselves as fellow students in the diversity process.

On the other hand, facilitating diversity sessions, especially program modules related to prejudice reduction and stereotype awareness, can be a very intense experience. Participants bring to the training room their own fears, frustrations, and assumptions on what the training will cover. Discussions can get out of hand easily. Diversity facilitators need to control the environment in order to minimize both legal risks for the organization they represent and excessive discomfort for participants.

All this makes it unwise to select a team of unseasoned trainers. Learning the specific challenges inherent to the diversity field is enough of a challenge without adding all the additional competencies required of any group facilitator.

At the very least, diversity facilitators need the following traits:

- strong awareness of their own prejudices and stereotypes, and the commitment to explore them continuously
- ability and willingness to practice what they preach
- comfort with their own cultural backgrounds and an understanding of how those backgrounds—as well as their own life experiences—affect their worldviews and their perceptions of other groups
- commitment to continuous learning and the ability to keep up with new developments in the field
- advanced leadership abilities
- advanced group facilitation skills
- emotional maturity.

It is crucial to emphasize the importance of this last characteristic. In this context, emotional maturity means the ability to keep one's emotions and feelings under control. Diversity facilitation requires a certain amount of emotional detachment. Facilitators who take into the training room uncontrolled resentment and anger toward certain groups or institutions are unlikely to be effective leaders. A good facilitator is able to listen respectfully to all points of view, even those that under normal circumstances would elicit a strongly negative or positive emotional reaction. If participants feel that only certain responses are accepted in the classroom, they are unlikely to engage in an open and honest dialogue.

Should organizations select diversity facilitators internally or hire an external consultant? As always, each option has pros and cons. A comparison of the strengths of external and internal facilitators is provided in Table 5–1.

Table 5–1

Comparative Strengths of Internal and External Facilitators

INTERNAL FACILITATORS	EXTERNAL FACILITATORS
◆ May be more cost effective, especially for large organizations ◆ Offers greater flexibility in scheduling because it is easier to schedule shorter sessions and organize programs with a modular format ◆ May have a better understanding of organization-specific issues ◆ May find it easier to guide participants in a discussion of the application of the learning ◆ May have easier access to organizational data and resources as needed	◆ May be more specialized and knowledgeable on diversity-specific topics ◆ May have more time to develop experiential processes and engaging programs ◆ May carry more credibility with certain groups within the organization ◆ May be perceived as more neutral and less involved in organization-specific politics ◆ May have better access to the top leadership and be able to make difficult recommendations

A possible option is to combine the best of both worlds: pair an external consultant with an internal trainer or leader so that both co-facilitate the session. This dual format brings the following advantages:

- Co-facilitation in diversity models to participants the kind of teamwork you are trying to encourage. Moreover, a facilitation team is particularly helpful if and when more intense dialogues and discussions arise during the training. Including an internal consultant reduces costs without sacrificing the synergy of a facilitation partnership.
- The external consultant brings expertise and programs honed by years of development and testing. The internal consultant is likely more able to effectively connect the program to issues and topics specific to the organization.

When the work of the external consultant is done, internal facilitators are able to continue guiding the learning through discussion, coaching, and small-group development activities. Because diversity development requires constant reinforcement it is unrealistic to expect all the work to be done by an external consultant. The external consultant can be called back periodically for more structured follow-up sessions.

A common practice when organizations select external or internal facilitators is to give preference to women and members of ethnic minority groups, or both. The traditional view is that people who have experienced some degree of discrimination will be more credible with the audience and able to speak from their own experience. This may be a flawed premise. Sound diversity facilitation is independent of a person's gender, ethnicity, race, or sexual orientation. Because influence tends to be higher among people who perceive themselves to be members of the same group, it might actually be helpful to include at least one member of the majority group in the training team.

The issue of influence is another reason for co-facilitation: With a pair of facilitators it is possible to include at least one minority-group and one majority-group member and thus model the kind of majority–minority relationship the organization would like to foster.

Even though training is not the *only* portion of a diversity development process, it is a key component and a very visible one. Diversity facilitators can easily make or break the success of a diversity initiative.

Planning Tips and Legal Pitfalls

Details are important. Everything related to diversity training initiatives—the quality of the facilitation; title and content of training; program length; and even the refreshments, training facility, and materials—sends a message. Programs should be carefully designed and put together, and they should convey to participants that the initiative is of vital importance.

Here is some key advice for planning and implementing a successful program:

- Do your homework. The complexity of diversity requires that some level of needs assessment be conducted before interventions are designed.
- Strive to bring the top leadership of the organization onboard. Leaders' input should be invited, welcomed, and honored from the start.
- Involve *everyone* in the organization. The goal of a truly multicultural organization will not be reached by a few people at the top working in isolation.
- Think *broadly.* Research (Holladay et al., 2003) has indicated that presenting a diversity program in terms of race alone tends to negative-

ly affect its success. Consider other diversity issues—gender, sexual orientation, weight, disabilities.

- Make at least a portion of the training common for all employees. One of the advantages of diversity and team-building initiatives is the creation of a common language with which to discuss factors that influence organizational success. The absence of a common process for all employees eliminates this benefit.
- Reinforce, reinforce, reinforce. Remember that diversity development has a strong attitude development component. Attitudes cannot be affected through short programs. As Willmore (2003, p. 30) humorously argued, "The performance problem didn't get that screwed up overnight, so it won't be solved overnight."
- Remember that diversity relations will not improve through training alone. All organizational reward systems—including compensation, promotions, recruitment, and even informal networks—must be aligned with your ultimate goal. People are more likely to observe and abide by those systems than by whatever is discussed or modeled during training.

Some pitfalls to avoid at all costs include

- very short programs and programs demonstrating minimal effort. Participants are quick to interpret such initiatives as an effort to "check the diversity box" or protect the organization from future lawsuits. Organizations should start diversity initiatives in earnest. It is fine, however, to divide a longer initiative into shorter modular sessions.
- selecting facilitators solely on the basis of their ethnicity, heritage, or culture. The fact that a person comes from a foreign country or is a member of a minority group should not automatically qualify him or her to conduct diversity facilitation.
- visible sloppiness in arranging the details of the training. Some organizations spend hundreds of thousands of dollars on large training initiatives and then choose to save on training location and refreshments. As a result, the success of the training is negatively affected and participants are resentful.

Legal pitfalls are particularly worrisome in dealing with diversity issues, so the wise program planner will involve the organization's legal team. In the event of a lawsuit, initiative designs as well as needs assessment reports could be subpoenaed and challenged (Amalfe and Akawie, 2004).

The involvement of legal counsel in all moments of a diversity process is essential and is presented last in this section for added emphasis. Concerned with the legal landmines associated with diversity initiatives, we asked Marshall Lachmann, an attorney from Dayton, Ohio, to offer comments and suggestions for this book.

Lachmann specifically addressed the issue of diversity audits, a common needs assessment process conducted prior to a diversity development initiative. From a business perspective, Lachmann said, diversity audits can be an excellent tool for uncovering organizational shortcomings. Legally, however, cultural audits could be a double-edged sword.

Many companies fear that if their audits uncover discrimination-related issues, the findings could be used against them in litigation. A good plaintiff's attorney, however, can also base a discrimination case on a company's *inaction.* Alternatively, a company could offer the defense that it did uncover problems but is trying to correct them.

Lachmann suggested that organizations keep in mind the following directives when undertaking a diversity audit:

- Undertake the audit only if the company is committed to seeing it through to the end. When an organization begins the process, any hope of claiming ignorance of a problem is greatly reduced and failure to act on any negative findings can be worse than having done nothing at all.
- Have in-house or outside legal counsel direct the audit. This enables the company to argue that it is protected by the attorney/client privilege. It is very important to limit access to any resulting documentation because the privilege can be lost if other people not under the umbrella of the attorney/client privilege see the reports.
- Make the reports as objective as possible using relevant statistical data and avoiding subjective comments.

We recommend that facilitators and managers receive a special orientation concerning their legal responsibilities as well as the potential legal pitfalls of diversity initiatives. It might, however, be a good idea to separate legal responsibility training modules from other modules that address prejudice reduction and diversity team building. If topics are grouped, the message received might be negative (that is, this training is merely a legal requirement to protect the organization) rather than positive (that is, this training is about success and reaching everyone's highest potential).

Group Selection, Room Arrangement, and Participant Materials

Because most of the activities described in this book require small-group discussions, we suggest that you locate a room where participants can be seated in groups of five or six people. It is ideal to plan sessions for groups of no more than 20 to 25 participants. When possible, plan your sessions around intact groups or groups of people who work together. Figure 5–1 offers a suggested arrangement and checklist.

To frame the diversity initiative positively and emphasize its importance to the organization, consider the following suggestions:

- Select a comfortable training room—one that is large enough for the group, well-lighted, and away from workplace distractions.
- Provide comfortable seating and tables.
- Develop and print attractive and professional participant materials.
- Have a supply of pens, pencils, and writing pads for all participants.
- Arrange for appropriate breaktime refreshments. You may also want to have water, sodas, coffee, and tea available in the room at all times. Try to select healthy snacks to keep participants alert. Sugary refreshments, although enjoyable, will only make participants tired and sluggish, especially if you are running a whole-day program.

Appreciative Inquiry and Diversity

A positive and upbeat message should permeate the entire diversity process. In modern society, however, Americans are sometimes "obsessed with learning from mistakes" (Hammond, 1998). Followers of Hammond's appreciative inquiry (AI) take an alternative route: They learn from *successes.*

AI is a development approach that focuses on the positive, rather than the negative. One of its premises is that in every situation something works. Because what people focus on tends to become their reality, focusing on what is working may increase the chances of further success.

Figure 5-1
Suggested Room Setup and Organization

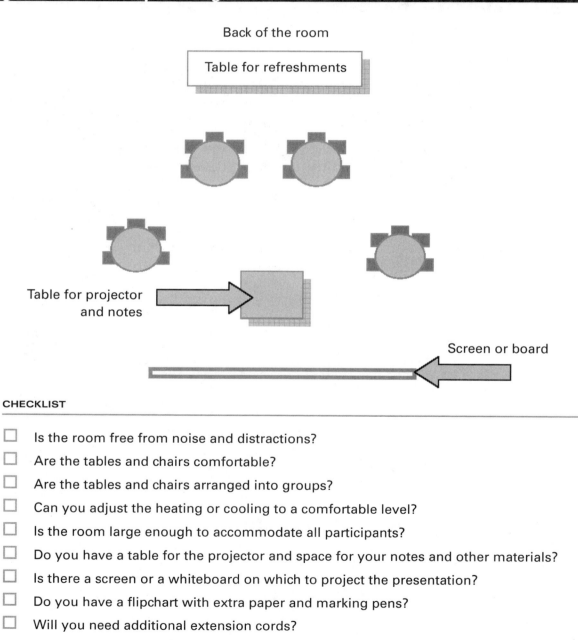

CHECKLIST

- ☐ Is the room free from noise and distractions?
- ☐ Are the tables and chairs comfortable?
- ☐ Are the tables and chairs arranged into groups?
- ☐ Can you adjust the heating or cooling to a comfortable level?
- ☐ Is the room large enough to accommodate all participants?
- ☐ Do you have a table for the projector and space for your notes and other materials?
- ☐ Is there a screen or a whiteboard on which to project the presentation?
- ☐ Do you have a flipchart with extra paper and marking pens?
- ☐ Will you need additional extension cords?

Trainers often facilitate team development sessions that run counter to AI advice. Remember those "problem-solving" sessions that quickly spiral down to a negative and unproductive blame game? Or staff meetings in which the mood quickly becomes so somber that it's a wonder anyone is able to do any decent work afterward? When participants focus narrowly on the negative side of an issue, their perception is blocked from picking up anything positive. They focus on problems and *all they see are problems.*

AI followers further believe that the language surrounding a topic influences the way people view that topic. Specifically, they argue that the wording and format of a specific message have a strong impact on the likelihood the message will be positively received. This belief is backed by research (Holladay et al., 2003) and could have practical implications for training design and facilitation.

The Conversity ideas presented in this book are partly based on AI. If participants focus first on what they have in common, they are more likely to selectively perceive commonalities rather than differences in their relationships.

AI messages are particularly relevant to diversity. For instance, when participants say, "I relate well to everyone," diversity facilitators commonly take that as a sign of naiveté. Facilitators then do their best to convince the poor, misguided souls that they are really too prejudiced to realize fully how *bad* they are. A more useful approach would be to ask participants questions such as these:

- When did you last have productive and enjoyable relationships with people who at first seemed to be different from you?
- What did you learn from that experience?
- How can you apply this learning to other situations involving differences?

It is vital at all costs to avoid negative terminology and negative discussions. Invite participants to "an advanced program that will improve even more our team work and success opportunities" rather than to "a program to reduce disrespectfulness in the workplace and comply with our latest EEOC guidelines." If it is important to discuss stereotyping in a diversity session, make sure that the stereotypes brought to the table are later disproved and substituted for by a more positive and realistic view of all human beings. If participants report having positive relationships with members of other groups, accept those reports as a success experience . . . and capitalize on the success.

What to Do Next

- Select your facilitation team.
- Decide whether to hire an external consulting partner. If so, conduct a search for that individual. It is wise to involve him or her early in the process.
- If approved by your legal counsel, conduct your cultural audit. You will need the results to plan your diversity interventions.
- Enlist help to ensure that all environmental details for your training (room location and comfort, refreshments, materials, and other details) will be attended to for maximum effectiveness.

◆◆◆

Are you ready to move on? Then take advantage of the contents of the following chapter. In it you will find a practical preparation guide and a road map for your diversity initiative, enabling you to track your progress through a step-by-step diversity development checklist. Chapter 6 also includes the rationale for the modular division of the program used in this book and module sequencing suggestions.

Chapter 6

Diversity Road Map

What's in This Chapter

- Step-by-step checklist to help you prepare for your diversity training program
- Summary of the contents of each training module and recommendations for sequencing them
- List of recommendations to increase the long-term impact of your programs

If you don't know where you're going, any road will take you there.
– Lewis Carroll (1832–1898), British author of *Alice in Wonderland*

You will find in this chapter a thorough step-by-step checklist to help you plan a comprehensive diversity initiative. The checklist includes suggestions for individual preparation, needs assessment, leadership involvement, facilitating team preparation, and even internal communication processes to frame the initiative in a positive light. Additionally, the chapter provides a rationale for our modular division, sequencing ideas and module descriptions, and valuable tips for extending the life and influence of your diversity initiative.

Step-by-Step Preparation

As your organization's diversity champion, you are a critical success factor. Your overall preparation is key. You can use Tool 6–1 (at the end of this chapter and on the accompanying CD-ROM) to identify possible tasks, develop your skills as a diversity trainer, and put together a thorough diversity development process. We recommend that you customize this list to include requirements specific to your organization.

Rationale for Our Modular Division

As discussed in previous chapters, diversity development is complex and requires the development of numerous competencies. It would be impossible to address all diversity competencies in a single program or to describe appropriate interventions in a single book. Because each competency set may require from two to four hours of intervention, a complete diversity development system might need several volumes of activities and presentation materials. This book focuses on basic and intermediate competencies, leading participants from the need to continuously find Conversity (Module 1: Out of the Box) to a greater awareness of personal prejudices and biases and of their impact on others (Module 4: Walking in Their Shoes). A workshop covering all of the competencies addressed by Modules 1 through 4 may be run in two days or divided into smaller sessions of two to four hours each. The latter format is recommended because the time between sessions enables participants to better digest and reinforce the content.

As you plan your system of diversity interventions, seriously consider the following directives:

- Train your managers first, and plan a managerial session to kick off the diversity initiative. Invite your legal counsel to this session.
- Ask for the collaboration of your legal counsel in discussing with managers their diversity-related legal responsibilities. If possible, schedule the legal discussion for a time other than the one set for the diversity development sessions. Even though legal issues are important, you don't want your entire diversity initiative to revolve around them.
- Customize the modules included in this book to your own needs and specific situation. Remember, however, that you must keep the original authors' names, company name, and the title and copyright notice of this book in your customized presentation and participant materials.
- Shorten modules if you must. By cutting certain slides and activities, you may be able to run all four modules in one day. Adult learners, however, may find it frustrating to be introduced to complex topics but not given sufficient time to process them. Ideally, move steadily and calmly through each module, making sure that you allot enough time for each activity.

Sequencing Ideas and Module Descriptions

The best option is to run each module individually, observing an interval of two to four weeks between trainings. If this is an impossible scenario, however, you can safely combine Modules 1 and 2 in one day and conduct Modules 3 and 4 in a second day. The complete agenda for each module is included in the following chapters as indicated below:

- **Module 1—Out of the Box** (chapter 8)

  Main topics: Group categorization, similarity bias, Conversity

  Time: 2.5–3 hours

  Synopsis: Social identity bias, or the tendency to give preference to members of one's own group, is introduced in this module through a lively simulation. Participants discover what happens when limited resources must be distributed among members of their own group and those of other groups. Later they discuss their reception of new group members and the impact of informal networks on professional success. Finally, the idea of Conversity is introduced and participants are encouraged to intentionally find commonalities with co-workers.

- **Module 2—Cultures and Values** (chapter 9)

  Main topics: Cultural and value differences, the impact of values on decision making

  Time: 3.5–4 hours

  Synopsis: Introduces participants to issues surrounding intercultural encounters. Topics include definition of culture, the importance of values, and value congruency (the relationship between personal and organizational values). Through experiential exercises and discussions, participants discover the impact of values on decision making and the challenges inherent to value differences in the workplace. Finally, participants use Conversity to reconcile value differences and practice asking nonjudgmental questions to more accurately interpret the behavior of co-workers.

- **Module 3—First Impressions** (chapter 10)

  Main topic: Stereotypes

  Time: 2–2.5 hours

Synopsis: Stereotypes are introduced and discussed. Participants gain awareness of hidden stereotypes and practice disproving them by sharing examples of situations that defy the stereotypes originally uncovered. Related topics discussed include the priming or awakening of stereotypes, the social and psychological functions of stereotypes, and the dangers of stereotype rigidity.

- **Module 4—Walking in Their Shoes** (chapter 11)

  Main topics: The origin of prejudices, subtle discrimination, the relationship between prejudiced attitudes and behaviors

  Time: 3.5–4 hours

  Synopsis: This is a powerful and sensitive module that helps participants come to terms with unconscious prejudices programmed throughout their entire lives. Participants gain awareness of the origins of their personal prejudices, experience the impact of prejudices and stereotypes on decision making, and test their assumptions on members of various groups.

At the end of each module we recommend that you ask each participant to personally commit to at least *one* thing he or she can do to apply what has been learned in the module. To increase their personal accountability, you may

- ask participants to share their personal commitment sheets with at least one other person
- ask them to share their personal commitment sheets with their supervisors
- develop an incentive program (giving small prizes, "company dollars," or other awards) to recognize and reward those who share their personal commitment plans and reach their personal goals.

It is ideal to develop a process in which participants discuss the contents of their personal commitment worksheets with their supervisors or a "Conversity partner" of their choosing after each session.

Making Training Stick

As we discussed in chapter 4, a common criticism of diversity initiatives is the absence of long-term data to substantiate their efficacy. This results not *only* from the lack of ROI studies. It may also result from the fact that most diversity initiatives *do not* have a long-term impact. Participants may be pleased with the intervention itself, and may then forget all about it within a few months.

Here are some possible solutions to this content drift:

- Divide the program into several modules so that each module will reinforce the contents of the previous one.
- Use the Personal Commitment learning activity you will find at the end of every module in this book. Participants are asked to sign and date their commitments. To build their accountability to your initiative we suggest you have participants schedule meetings with their managers to discuss these commitments. Of course this process requires that managers (a) strongly support the process and (b) participate in training before their employees. Otherwise participants will quickly realize that the personal commitment is only a formality.
- Tie organizational rewards to diversity-related goals and to the completion of individual Personal Commitment plans. Especially remember to reward managers for their commitment to the process and their support in coaching in diversity program contents those workers whom they supervise.

Above all, remember the earlier discussion on appreciative inquiry and diversity (chapter 5). All processes pertaining to the diversity initiative should continuously remind people of a positive experience. Tap into in-house or outside marketing gurus and consider devising an ongoing and exciting marketing campaign to sustain your diversity initiative.

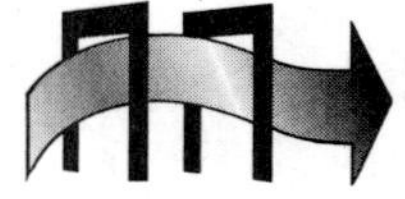

What to Do Next

- Read through Tool 6–1: Preparation Checklist and customize it to match the objectives and needs of your organization.
- Meet with your legal counsel to discuss how to run a managerial orientation session to prepare your managers to handle diversity-related legal issues.
- Go through Modules 1, 2, 3, and 4 (chapters 8 through 11) and decide which of those modules you will run at your organization.
- Plan a strategy to "make learning stick."

◆◆◆

The full commitment of the top leadership of your organization often means the difference between the success and the failure of your diversity initiative. For starters you need to bring your leaders onboard. The next chapter gives you a detailed description of a leadership presentation designed to do just that.

Tool 6–1

Preparation Checklist for the Conversity Development System

PART I: INDIVIDUAL DEVELOPMENT AND SELF-AWARENESS

- [ ] Read chapters 1–5 of this workbook.
- [ ] Complete a self-awareness assessment (Assessment 13–1).
- [ ] Participate in a diversity training program.
- [ ] Attend diversity conferences, as available.
- [ ] Formulate a personal development action plan.

PART II: LEADERSHIP INVOLVEMENT

- [ ] If possible, invite others to collaborate on your internal needs assessment.
- [ ] Collect *preliminary* data on your organization. More thorough research may be conducted in the needs analysis phase, after resources are allotted for this end with the support of your organization's leadership. Possible areas of investigation include the following:
    - levels of litigation, EEOC claims, and/or harassment complaints
    - turnover data (Do turnover levels vary according to employee membership in a certain group?)
    - existing employee satisfaction survey results (Are there any trends or group-specific concerns?)
    - relationship between ethnic/cultural/gender diversity of the community you serve and that of your employees and leadership
    - customer analysis (Does your organization reach all groups within your target geographic area?)
    - customer satisfaction survey results (Are there any trends or group-specific concerns?)
    - global marketing (Do you sell your products or services abroad? If not, could you?)
    - reward systems (How are people promoted? How do they receive raises? How competitive is the general environment?)
    - quality and productivity data.
- [ ] Read chapter 7 in preparation for a presentation to your organization's leadership.
- [ ] Customize the leadership presentation according to internal data collected, time available, and audience in attendance.
- [ ] Run the leadership presentation.

Continued on next page

Tool 6–1, continued

Preparation Checklist for the Conversity Development System

- ☐ Select a task force to serve as an advisory board and working committee throughout the diversity development process. Be certain to involve leaders as appropriate. Diversity development works best with the involvement of as many organizational members as feasible.
- ☐ Run a leadership focus group to help
    - generate ideas for the initiative
    - discuss systemic changes to support the initiative (consider areas such as leadership development, recruitment, compensation, reward systems, and the like)
    - review mission, vision, and goals, connecting these to diversity development needs
    - decide on the breadth of the needs assessment according to resources available.

PART III: NEEDS ASSESSMENT

- ☐ Consider the topics suggested in your preliminary research: Which ones warrant further study?
- ☐ Decide on at least two methods of information gathering (that is, surveys, interviews, focus groups, analysis of company documents, and so forth).
- ☐ Identify the main stakeholder groups at your organization.
- ☐ Research main culture-specific practices of these groups.
- ☐ Have legal counsel review all needs analysis plans and materials.
- ☐ Divide the needs assessment work load appropriately and run the needs assessment.
- ☐ Analyze results.

PART IV: PROGRAM DEVELOPMENT AND EVALUATION DESIGN

- ☐ Decide whether all issues revealed through your needs analysis are addressed by the modules included in this book. (All of the competencies covered in Modules 1 through 4 are listed in chapter 4.)
- ☐ Read chapters 8 through 11.
- ☐ Decide how you are going to track your progress.
- ☐ Develop or procure evaluation systems and materials.
- ☐ Customize presentations and program materials according to your specific needs. Develop or procure additional materials if appropriate.

Continued on next page

Tool 6–1, continued

Preparation Checklist for the Conversity Development System

Design Tip: Make sure that your programs and the goals to be measured through your evaluation *match.* If, for instance, your objective is to develop conflict resolution skills, the assessment, presentation, and practice of such skills need be part of the program. If you would like to reduce customer complaints, customer service discussions must be added to the diversity-specific processes suggested in this book. (If needed, procure additional materials such as the ones provided by other titles in the ASTD Trainer's WorkShop Series.)

- ☐ Design incentive systems that connect completion of program activities and action plans to organizational rewards.
- ☐ Decide on appropriate reinforcement and follow-up processes.
- ☐ Have legal counsel review all instructional materials and training and incentive plans.

PART V: PREPARING YOUR PILOT PROGRAM

- ☐ Print participant materials.
- ☐ Invite a small group of workers to pilot-test your first workshop.
- ☐ Lead a focus-group discussion with members of the pilot group to suggest improvements to the training.
- ☐ Revise the workshop according to the recommendations of the focus group. Ask your legal counsel to approve any significant changes made.

PART VI: PREPARING THE FACILITATING TEAM

- ☐ Determine your selection criteria for facilitators.
- ☐ Design your train-the-trainer process.
- ☐ Train your facilitators.
- ☐ Plan the pilot process so as to enable each facilitator to first observe the workshops they are expected to run. For instance, you may have two facilitators observe you as you run the first program. Other facilitators may later observe those first two people trained.
- ☐ Have new trainers co-facilitate a session with you.
- ☐ Plan and implement a continuous improvement/feedback process for facilitators.
- ☐ Follow this sequence for each training module you choose to include.

PART VII: MARKETING

- ☐ Involve the organization's marketing division to help design promotional and campaign materials in support of your diversity development programs.

Chapter 7

Getting Leadership Onboard

What's in This Chapter?

- Advice on preparation steps before conducting a leadership diversity presentation
- Detailed presentation to members of the leadership team, including the objectives, a list of materials, and a sample step-by-step agenda of activities

Leadership and learning are indispensable to each other.

–John F. Kennedy (1917–1963),
35th president of the United States

The impact of any training initiative is greatly influenced by the support provided by the key leadership of the organization. This is especially true in diversity development efforts where interventions need to be lengthier (and thus costlier), include follow-up processes, and may have a subtle and hard-to-quantify result.

This chapter will help you prepare to conduct a leadership presentation designed to get key organization executives onboard. It provides ideas to aid in your preparation and a scripted one-hour presentation accompanied by PowerPoint slides.

Preparation Ideas

Here are four ideas to consider as you prepare your presentation:

1. Because this presentation includes a summary of the main concepts introduced in this book, you will find it useful to thoroughly read the previous chapters during your preparation.

2. Support from the top is vital for the success of any diversity initiative. Employees will quickly perceive whether the initiative is for real, depending on overt or subtle messages they receive from managers. On the other hand, managers are understandably more likely to endorse initiatives that carry weight in the main offices. Few people are interested in lost causes.

3. The way a diversity initiative is packaged matters and affects the way it is likely to be received by others. A diversity champion's passion, commitment, knowledge, and determination carry significant weight as well. If you are your organization's diversity champion, this presentation is a good chance to package diversity development in a positive, straightforward, and credible way.

4. Do your homework. The PowerPoint presentation and the instructions included in this chapter are starting points, but you will need to conduct your own company-specific research. Consult Tool 6–1: Preparation Checklist for the Conversity Development System for possible needs assessment areas.

The presentation included in this chapter should be run in approximately two hours. If you need to reduce the presentation length, we suggest that you

- reduce the number of slides presented in the "Fact or Fiction" section (slides 7–4 through 7–11) or delete those slides and replace them with your own customized business case using slide 7–12.
- eliminate the Conversity pair discussion on slide 7–14.
- prior to this presentation, hold meetings with your diversity task force or other stakeholders in the diversity process to discuss a strategy for a return-on-expectations (slide 7–13) and a leadership commitment process (slide 7–24) that will be presented to the top leadership.

Training Objectives for Your Leadership Presentation

The objectives for this presentation to the organization's leadership are to help leaders

- differentiate myth from fact in the business case for diversity
- agree on a return-on-expectations strategy

- define, practice, and discuss the rationale for and the value of the Conversity philosophy
- agree on the next step to take toward a thorough diversity development system that will benefit the organization.

Materials

There are a number of things you will need to facilitate this presentation. The list below will help you prepare properly.

For the instructor:

- Projector, screen, and computer for running the PowerPoint presentation
- PowerPoint slides 7–1 through 7–24 (*Leadership.ppt* on the CD; thumbnail copies of the slides appear at the end of this chapter)

For the participants:

- Copies of PowerPoint slides 7–1 through 7–24. Black-and-white versions of the slides can be printed from the overhead masters file, *Leadership.pps,* on the CD. (We suggest that you print three slides per page.)
- Training Instrument 13–1: Introducing Conversity
- Training Instrument 13–2: Next Steps
- Copies of relevant organization-specific documentation uncovered in your preparation for this session

Using the CD

Materials for the leadership presentation are provided in this workbook and as electronic files on the accompanying CD. To access the electronic files, insert the CD and click on the appropriate Adobe .pdf or PowerPoint .ppt/.pps files. Further directions and help using the files can be found in the appendix, "Using the Compact Disc," at the back of this workbook.

It's important that you review all of the slides as part of your preparation for the session. At that time you should plan explanations and examples for concepts presented in the slides.

As with all the other materials in this book, you may adapt the slides and handouts as long as you include in all your presentation materials the authors' names, company name, title of this book, and the copyright information.

Leadership Presentation Sample Agenda

8:00 a.m. Welcome and introductions (5 minutes)

Display slide 7–1. Welcome participants to the session and thank them for taking part. If needed and appropriate, allow for brief personal introductions.

8:05 Identify the purpose of the presentation (5 minutes)

Display slide 7–2 and let participants read the quote. Tell them they are here to discuss the benefits of a diversity initiative for their organization and to design their own diversity road map. Explain that you will share with them the latest research on the topic and make some suggestions for implementing a thorough diversity development system.

8:10 Present the agenda (5 minutes)

Display slide 7–3. Briefly enumerate the contents of the presentation. Here are some comments you may want to make for each bullet on slide 7–3:

- Fact or Fiction: *I will share with you what is traditionally presented as "The Business Case for Diversity" and help you differentiate fact from fiction.*
- Return-on-Expectations: *We will discuss as a group some appropriate ways to measure our progress.*
- Introducing Conversity: *Research indicates that diversity development works best if it is based on common ground. I will share a new diversity approach that I am confident will work at our organization.*
- Toward Multiculturalism: *I will share the best practices for a thorough diversity development system. We will agree together on our next steps and define how the lead-*

ership of our organization will demonstrate its full commitment to the diversity initiative.

8:15 Traditional arguments for the business case for diversity (15 minutes)

Display slide 7–4. Say: *These five arguments form the traditional business case for diversity. As I go through each of them individually, I'll first ask you to give me your opinions: Do you think the argument is fact, fiction, or a combination of both?*

Display slides 7–5 through 7–11. First display only the title of each slide. Ask participants to guess whether the argument identified in the title is fact or fiction. Then reveal the bullet points under each title and use the slide animation to explain whether each argument is valid (fact) or a myth (fiction).

8:30 Present organization-specific data to support the business case (20 minutes)

Display slide 7–12. Say: *We have now analyzed the typical business case for diversity and differentiated myth from fact. However, the business case that matters is* our *business case.*

At this point, distribute copies of relevant data from your internal research and facilitate a discussion on the importance of diversity for *your* organization.

8:50 Define the organization's expectations (20 minutes)

Display slide 7–13. Explain that it is important to track your progress and continuously improve your processes. Suggest that an exact return-on-investment study is tricky because of possible biases such as these:

- **Time:** When groups work together for some time they tend to improve their processes. Longevity is the best friend of work groups, and turnover is their greatest enemy.
- **Multiple variables:** Diversity relations are affected not only by diversity training but also by issues such as turnover, competition, leadership styles, and even the company's current level of success.

- **Legal concerns:** Add that it is vital to involve the organization's legal counsel in the entire process, including any preliminary cultural audit that is planned.

Explain that even though biases make "certainty" an impossibility in any evaluation study, the group shouldn't be discouraged from planning a return-on-expectations process based on the organization's expectations of the diversity initiative. Remind participants that diversity development is a very-long-term process and it is unrealistic to expect quick results.

Lead a discussion on the objectives for a diversity initiative in your organization. (You will use the objectives defined by this discussion later when you plan your evaluation processes.)

9:10 Introduce Conversity (10 minutes)

Display slide 7–14. Explain that participants will next have the opportunity to sample an activity that is part of a basic diversity development module.

Distribute a copy of Training Instrument 13–1: Introducing Conversity to each participant.

Ask them to form pairs and groups of three and discuss similarities. Encourage participants to go beyond the obvious and search for commonalities they might not have been aware of before.

After five minutes of discussion, facilitate a quick review of some of the similarities found.

9:20 Define Conversity (5 minutes)

Display slides 7–15 and 7–16. Paraphrase the contents of slide 7–16 to define Conversity.

9:25 Identify the benefits of Conversity (5 minutes)

Display slide 7–17. Facilitate a quick discussion of the benefits of Conversity exercises. Ask the following question: Why do you think it would be beneficial to include exercises like this in a diversity initiative? Alternatively (if you have a larger group), have small groups of leaders answer the question at the bottom of Training Instrument 13–1.

9:30 Explain categorization and similarity bias (5 minutes)

Display slides 7–18 and 7–19 and paraphrase their contents to explain the concepts of categorization and similarity bias.

Display slides 7–20 and 7–21. Use their contents to explain that because of categorization and similarity bias, it is very important to include in the diversity initiative some strong team-building and Conversity processes that help people find similarities and enable them to feel that they belong to the same group.

9:35 Identify best practices (10 minutes)

Display slide 7–22. Go through the bullet points to present best practices for a complete diversity initiative.

Note: The inclusion of attitude training in diversity initiatives, as suggested in the third bullet of slide 7–22, is controversial. Some people believe that organizational initiatives should address behaviors only. The authors' view is that because modern racism is often subtle, it is important to address the attitudes behind discriminatory behaviors.

9:45 Define the organizational culture that supports diversity development (5 minutes)

Display slide 7–23. Explain that diversity relations are influenced not only by training but also by the entire system of the organization. Systemic factors include whether the organization encourages competition over collaboration, how rewards are distributed, the style of leadership practiced, and whether equality or hierarchy is part of the culture. An organization that encourages collaboration, makes rewards contingent on teamwork, exhibits participative management styles, and emphasizes equality is more likely to be successful in its diversity efforts.

9:50 Identify next steps (20 minutes)

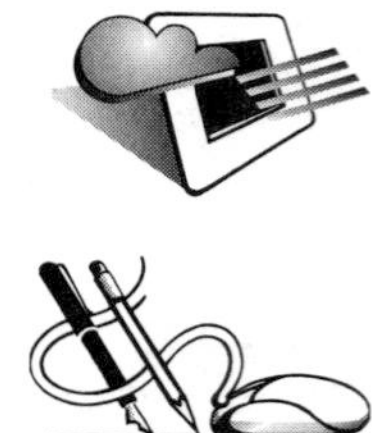

Display slide 7–24 and distribute a copy of Training Instrument 13–2: Next Steps to each participant.

Use the questions in the handout and on the slide to facilitate a discussion of the implications of your presentation content to the organization. Then help participants determine the next steps for the diversity development initiative.

10:10 Close (5 minutes)

Commend participants for the work they've done during the session and thank them for their commitment to developing diversity in your organization.

What to Do Next

- Meet with your task force and with other relevant stakeholders to gather information for the Return-on-Expectations and Leadership Commitment portions of the leadership presentation.
- Customize as needed the leadership presentation included here.
- Collect and/or produce all necessary materials, including participant handouts.
- Arrange meeting logistics—location, refreshments, audiovisual equipment, and so forth.
- Rehearse your presentation with someone you trust to give you honest feedback.
- Run the leadership presentation with the top leaders of your organization.

◆◆◆

The first step of a diversity development process is to help participants find common ground. Conversity is the focus of the first module, which is thoroughly describe in chapter 8. Get ready to start your diversity initiative in a fun and highly positive light!

Slide 7–1

Diversity Leadership

The Business Case

Cris Wildermuth, M.Ed.
Susan D. Gray, PHR

Slide 7–2

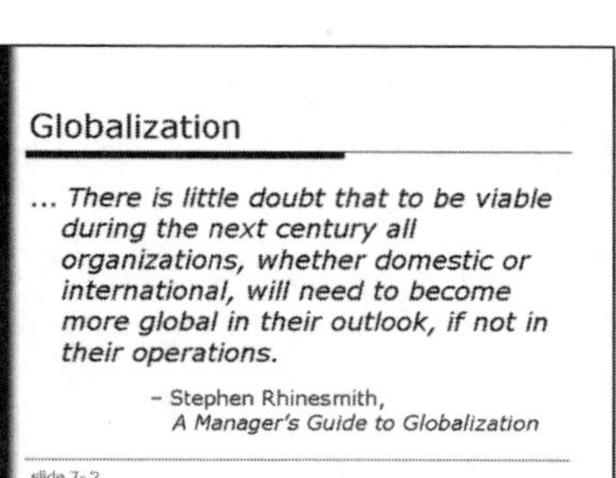

Globalization
... There is little doubt that to be viable during the next century all organizations, whether domestic or international, will need to become more global in their outlook, if not in their operations.
– Stephen Rhinesmith,
A Manager's Guide to Globalization
slide 7- 2

Slide 7–3

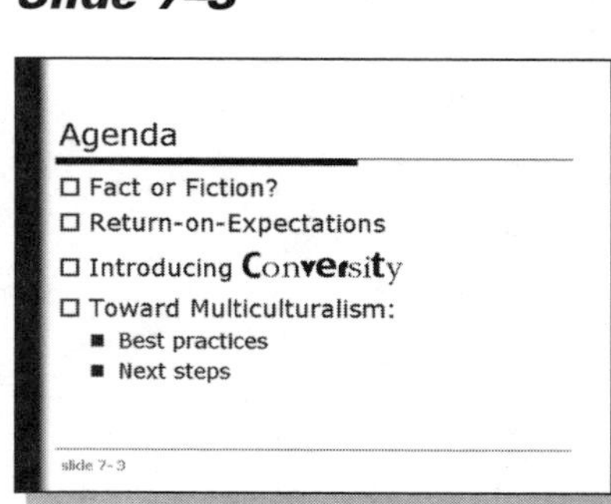

Agenda
☐ Fact or Fiction?
☐ Return-on-Expectations
☐ Introducing Conversity
☐ Toward Multiculturalism:
■ Best practices
■ Next steps
slide 7- 3

Slide 7–4

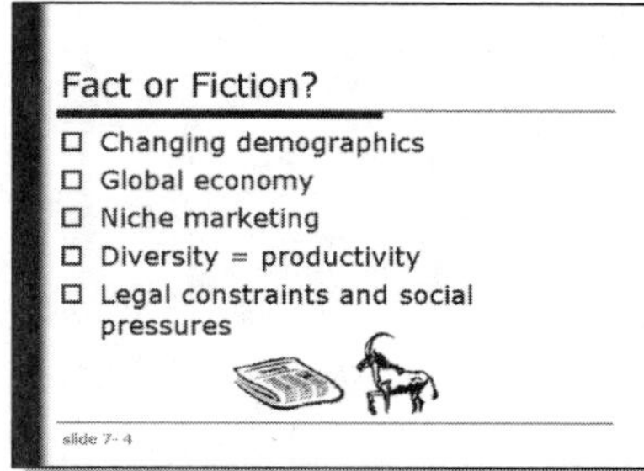

Fact or Fiction?
☐ Changing demographics
☐ Global economy
☐ Niche marketing
☐ Diversity = productivity
☐ Legal constraints and social pressures
slide 7- 4

Slide 7–5

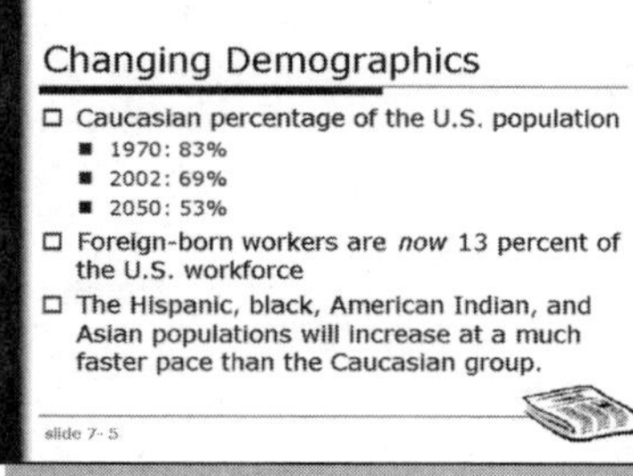

Changing Demographics
☐ Caucasian percentage of the U.S. population
■ 1970: 83%
■ 2002: 69%
■ 2050: 53%
☐ Foreign-born workers are now 13 percent of the U.S. workforce
☐ The Hispanic, black, American Indian, and Asian populations will increase at a much faster pace than the Caucasian group.
slide 7- 5

Slide 7–6

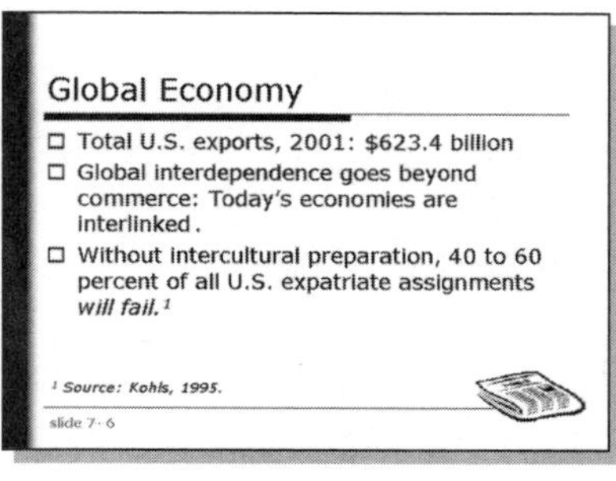

Global Economy
☐ Total U.S. exports, 2001: $623.4 billion
☐ Global interdependence goes beyond commerce: Today's economies are interlinked.
☐ Without intercultural preparation, 40 to 60 percent of all U.S. expatriate assignments will fail.1
1 Source: Kohls, 1995.
slide 7- 6

Slide 7–7

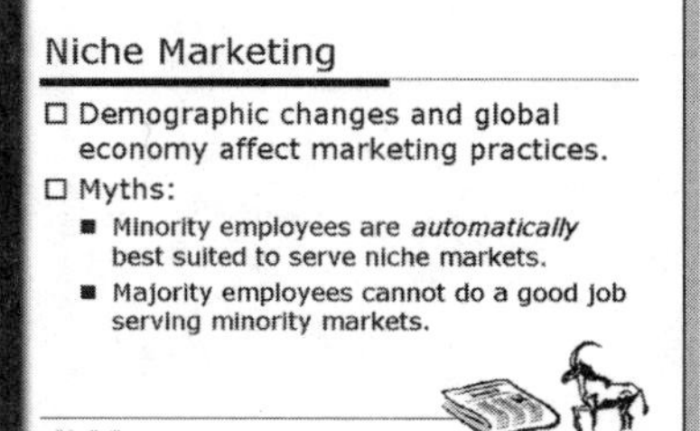

Niche Marketing
☐ Demographic changes and global economy affect marketing practices.
☐ Myths:
■ Minority employees are automatically best suited to serve niche markets.
■ Majority employees cannot do a good job serving minority markets.
slide 7- 7

Slide 7–8

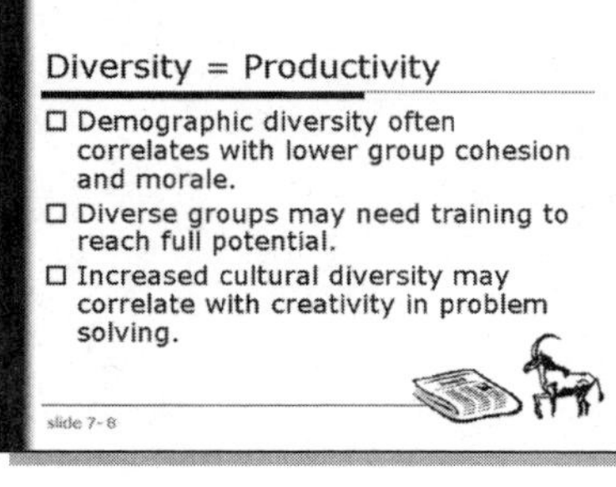

Diversity = Productivity
☐ Demographic diversity often correlates with lower group cohesion and morale.
☐ Diverse groups may need training to reach full potential.
☐ Increased cultural diversity may correlate with creativity in problem solving.
slide 7- 8

Slide 7–9

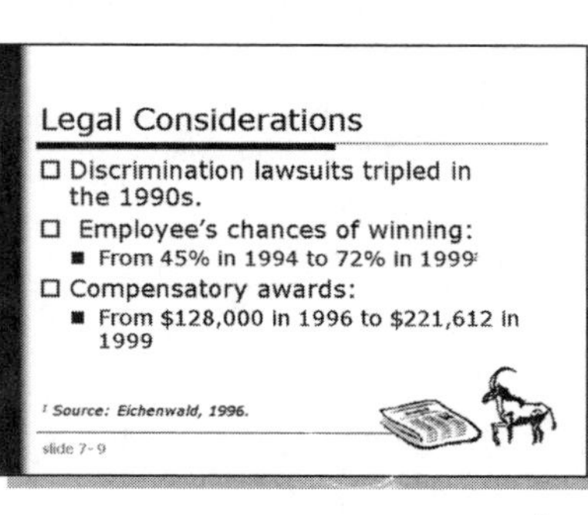

Legal Considerations
☐ Discrimination lawsuits tripled in the 1990s.
☐ Employee's chances of winning:
■ From 45% in 1994 to 72% in 19991
☐ Compensatory awards:
■ From $128,000 in 1996 to $221,612 in 1999
1 Source: Eichenwald, 1996.
slide 7- 9

Slide 7–10

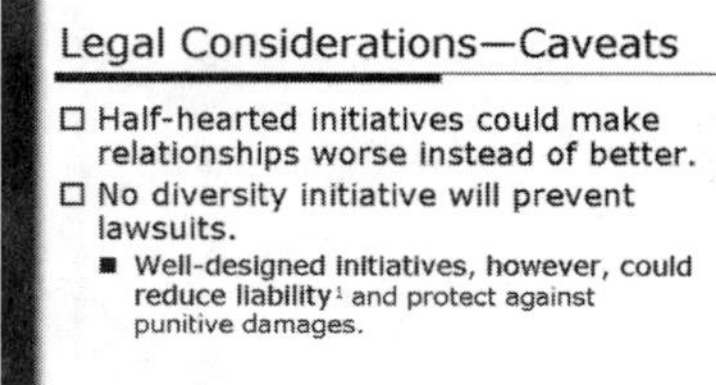

Legal Considerations—Caveats
☐ Half-hearted initiatives could make relationships worse instead of better.
☐ No diversity initiative will prevent lawsuits.
■ Well-designed initiatives, however, could reduce liability1 and protect against punitive damages.
1 Source: Prince, 2003.
slide 7- 10

Slide 7–11

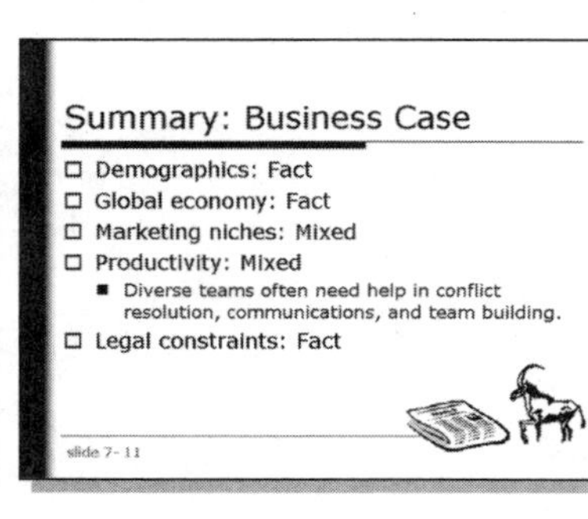

Summary: Business Case
☐ Demographics: Fact
☐ Global economy: Fact
☐ Marketing niches: Mixed
☐ Productivity: Mixed
■ Diverse teams often need help in conflict resolution, communications, and team building.
☐ Legal constraints: Fact
slide 7- 11

Slide 7–12

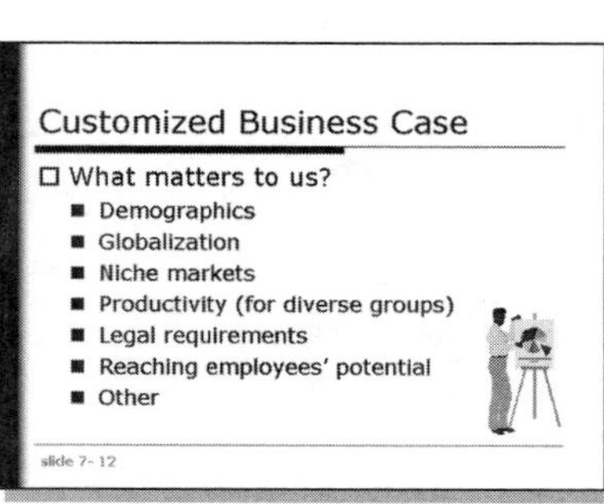

Customized Business Case
☐ What matters to us?
■ Demographics
■ Globalization
■ Niche markets
■ Productivity (for diverse groups)
■ Legal requirements
■ Reaching employees' potential
■ Other
slide 7- 12

Slide 7–13

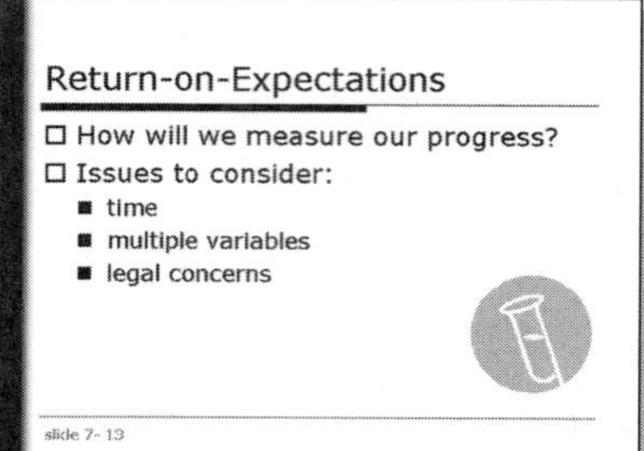

Return-on-Expectations
☐ How will we measure our progress?
☐ Issues to consider:
■ time
■ multiple variables
■ legal concerns
slide 7- 13

Slide 7–14

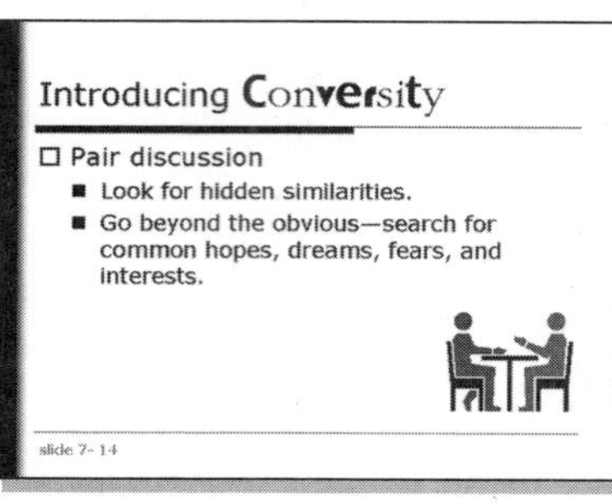

Introducing Conversity
☐ Pair discussion
■ Look for hidden similarities.
■ Go beyond the obvious—search for common hopes, dreams, fears, and interests.
slide 7- 14

Slide 7–15

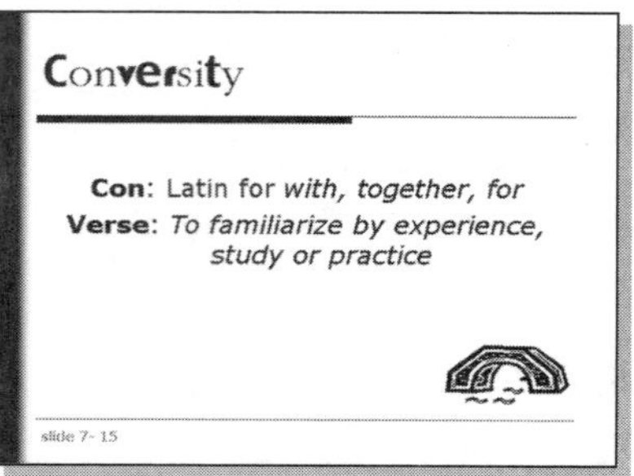

Conversity
Con: Latin for with, together, for
Verse: To familiarize by experience, study or practice
slide 7- 15

Slide 7–16

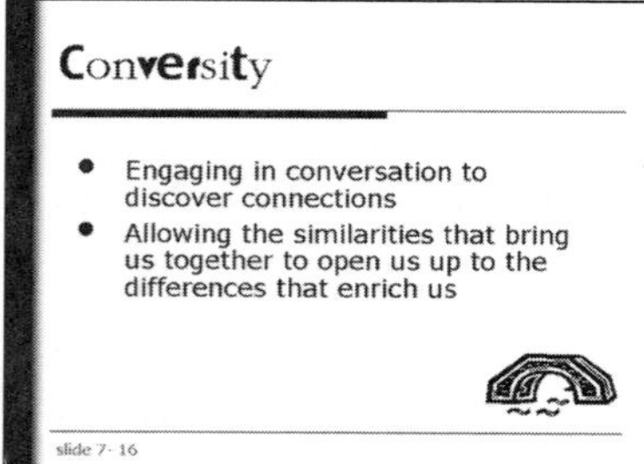

Conversity
• Engaging in conversation to discover connections
• Allowing the similarities that bring us together to open us up to the differences that enrich us
slide 7- 16

Slide 7–17

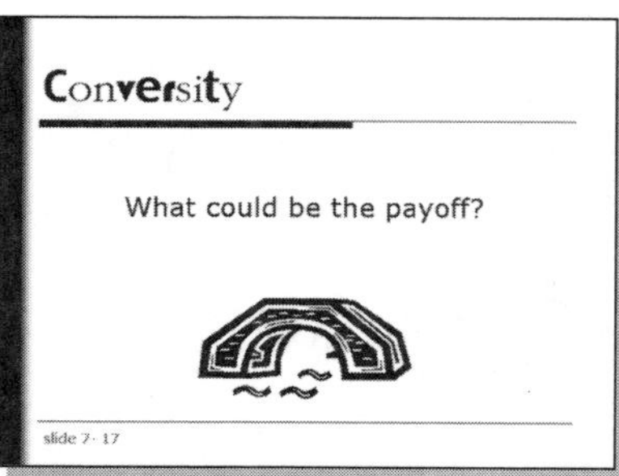

Conversity
What could be the payoff?
slide 7- 17

Slide 7–18

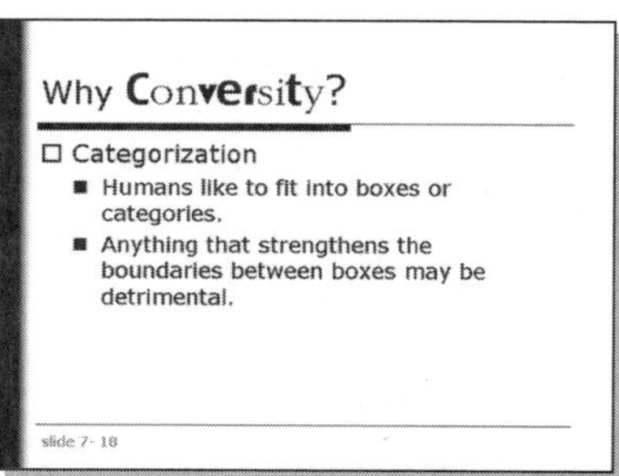

Why Conversity?
☐ Categorization
■ Humans like to fit into boxes or categories.
■ Anything that strengthens the boundaries between boxes may be detrimental.
slide 7- 18

Slide 7–19

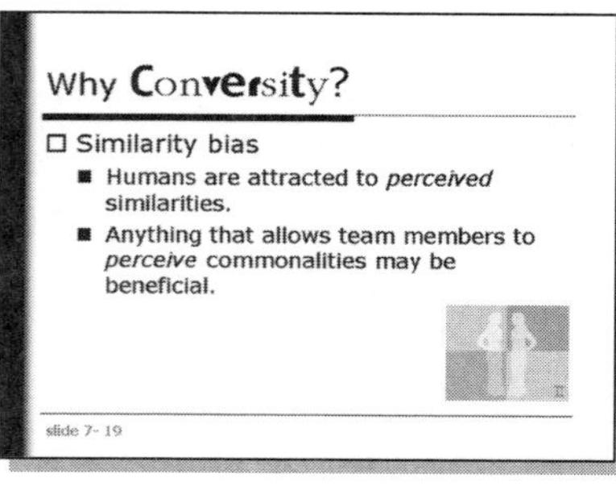

Why Conversity?
☐ Similarity bias
■ Humans are attracted to perceived similarities.
■ Anything that allows team members to perceive commonalities may be beneficial.
slide 7- 19

Slide 7–20

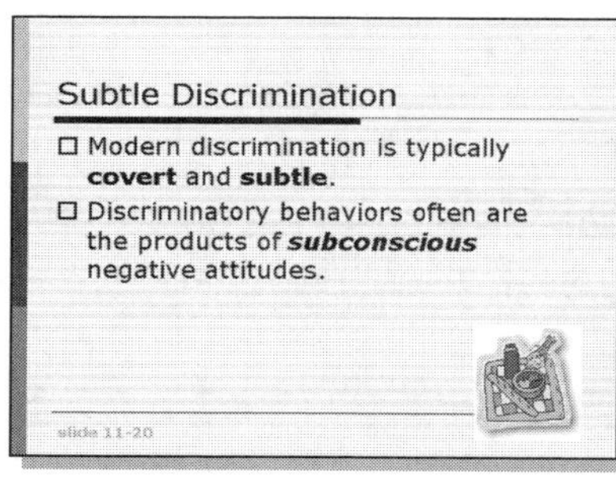

Subtle Discrimination
☐ Modern discrimination is typically covert and subtle.
☐ Discriminatory behaviors often are the products of subconscious negative attitudes.
slide 11-20

Slide 7–21

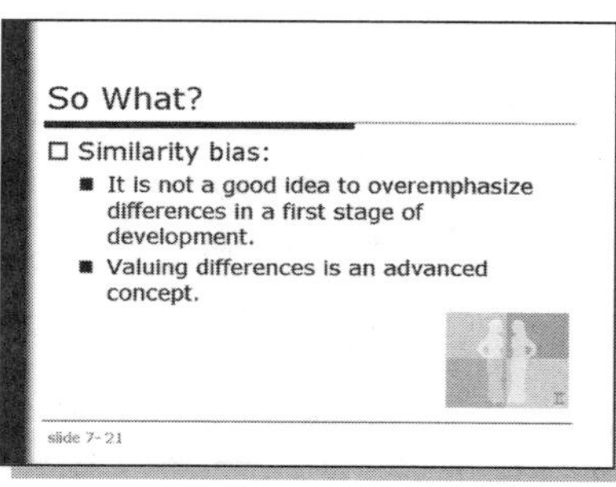

So What?
☐ Similarity bias:
■ It is not a good idea to overemphasize differences in a first stage of development.
■ Valuing differences is an advanced concept.
slide 7- 21

Slide 7–22

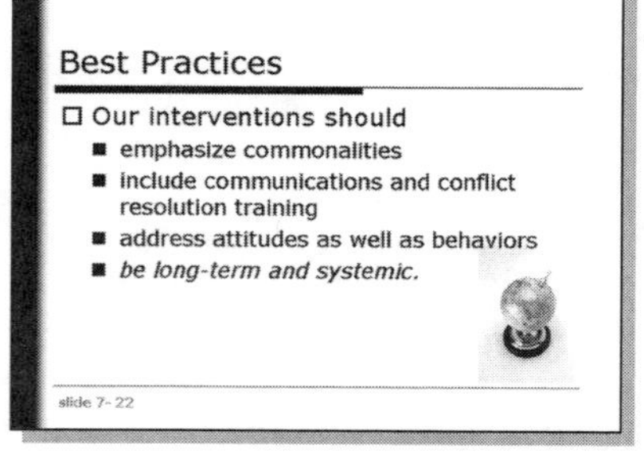

Best Practices
☐ Our interventions should
■ emphasize commonalities
■ include communications and conflict resolution training
■ address attitudes as well as behaviors
■ be long-term and systemic.
slide 7- 22

Slide 7–23

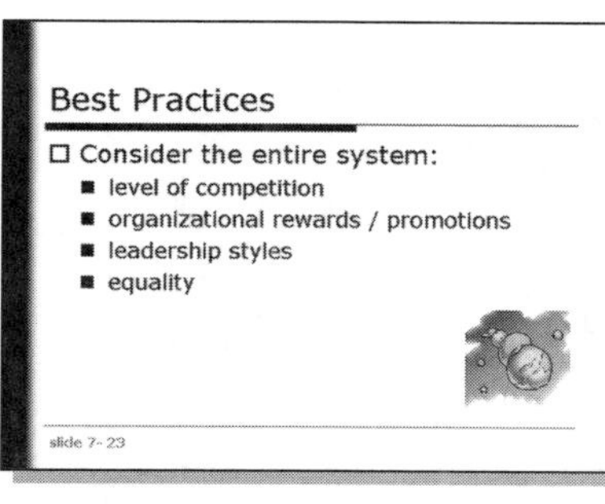

Best Practices
☐ Consider the entire system:
■ level of competition
■ organizational rewards / promotions
■ leadership styles
■ equality
slide 7- 23

Slide 7–24

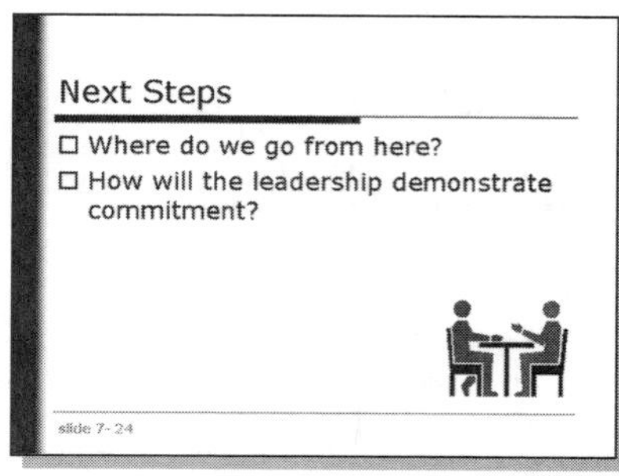

Next Steps
☐ Where do we go from here?
☐ How will the leadership demonstrate commitment?
slide 7- 24

Chapter 8

Module 1: Out of the Box

What's in This Chapter?

- Objectives for the three-hour introductory module
- Discussion of the legal safety of the instructional activities contained in the module
- List of materials for the facilitator and the participants
- Sample program agenda

Never doubt that a small group of thoughtful, committed citizens can change the world. Indeed, it is the only thing that ever has.
– Margaret Mead (1901–1978), U.S. anthropologist

Module 1: Out of the Box works well on its own if the time available for training is limited. It is positive and upbeat, is unlikely to generate negative feelings, and will introduce the power of Conversity to your teams.

If your organization is experiencing serious diversity-related problems, however, this module is not enough. It is a good first step to establishing a common ground of trust and preparing employees for more intensive modules.

This chapter includes all the instructions you'll need to conduct a training with this module. The session will last about three hours.

All instructions included in this module assume you will have a group of 20 participants, subdivided into four small groups of five members. If your group size is different, please adjust the quantities of materials accordingly.

If you plan to present more modules after this one, make sure participants know how to register for them. It is useful to run all modules with the same group and the same facilitator(s) so that trust and comfort levels within the class gradually improve.

How Safe Is Module 1?

Diversity programs include discussions of sensitive topics. Despite your best efforts, no diversity process is 100 percent safe, especially if you consider that trainer–participant discussions are not privileged and can be subpoenaed during litigation. For these reasons, all activities, including the ones described here and in the chapters that follow, should be approved by your organization's legal counsel.

Whether a particular activity is right for your organization depends on numerous factors:

- the organizational environment
- the number of employees
- the general management style.

Many organizations choose to combine managers and employees in the same diversity sessions. This approach may be beneficial because employees and managers may have few other opportunities to interact and discuss issues of importance to everyone. It is wise, however, to hold a special managerial orientation session prior to the beginning of your initiative. Ideally, this session should be facilitated or co-facilitated by a labor lawyer. It is important that managers understand that during the training they will be closely watched by employees. Managers' respectful behaviors and positive attitudes toward the training and the facilitator are likely to have a significant effect on the success of the program. Inappropriate comments or behaviors, on the other hand, are unlikely to be forgotten.

Your managers are agents of the organization. Their responsibilities—and potential liabilities—are greater than those of nonmanagerial personnel. Even if you choose to run a shorter program for employees, the process should be intensified for managers. The leadership of the organization, including middle managers and line leaders, must be 100 percent onboard before any diversity-related initiative begins.

Training Objectives

The objectives for Module 1 are to help participants

- describe the impact of categorization on human relationships
- discuss the impact of categorization on informal professional networks and professional success

- use Conversity techniques to actively seek common ground with members of other groups.

Materials

There are several things you will need to facilitate this presentation. The list below will help you prepare properly.

For the instructor:

- 20 paper clips or other colorful objects in four different colors
- Two additional jars of 20 paper clips each (total of 40 paper clips or two times the number of participants)
- Learning Activity 12–1: The P^2C^2 Challenge, Parts I and II
- Learning Activity 12–2: Seeking Connections
- Learning Activity 12–3: Personal Commitment
- Projector, screen, and computer for running the PowerPoint presentation
- PowerPoint slides 8–1 through 8–17 (*Module 1.ppt* on the CD; thumbnail copies of the slides appear at the end of this chapter)

For the participants:

- Training Instrument 13–1: Introducing Conversity
- Training Instrument 13–3: Welcome to P^2C^2
- Training Instrument 13–4: Windfall!
- Training Instrument 13–5: The P^2C^2 Challenge
- Training Instrument 13–6: Personal Commitment Worksheet
- Assessment 13–2: Sample Level 1 Evaluation

Using the CD

Materials for this training session are provided in this workbook and as electronic files on the accompanying CD. To access the electronic files, insert the CD and click on the appropriate Adobe .pdf or PowerPoint .ppt/.pps files. Further directions and help using the files can be found in the appendix, "Using the Compact Disc," at the back of this workbook.

It's important that you review all of the slides as part of your preparation for the workshop. At that time you should plan explanations and examples for concepts presented in the slides.

As with all the other materials in this book, you may adapt the slides and handouts as long as you include in all your presentation materials the authors' names, company name, title of this book, and copyright information.

Module 1 Sample Agenda

8:00 a.m. Welcome and introductions (15 minutes)

Display slide 8–1. Welcome the participants and thank them for taking part in the training session.

Display slide 8–2. Ask participants to introduce themselves to the group, using something they have in their wallets, pockets, or purses. It may be helpful to give them examples: family photos, good-luck items, library cards, keys. Ask them to show their selected object as they introduce themselves and explain what makes it important to them.

Time-saving alternative: Ask participants to do these introductions within their own small groups.

8:15 Present the agenda (5 minutes)

Display slide 8–3. Briefly enumerate the agenda items for the day. Distribute one copy of each training instrument to every participant.

8:20 Learning Activity 12–1: The P^2C^2 Challenge, Part I (40 minutes)

9:00 Learning Activity 12–1: The P^2C^2 Challenge, Part II (50 minutes)

The lesson to be learned in this exercise is that when competition is established, groups try to reserve available resources for their own members. Don't explain this lesson to the class until the activity has been completed.

9:50 Break (10 minutes)

10:00 Discussion about categorization (10 minutes)

Display slide 8–10. Discuss questions on the slide. You are making the case for categorization—the human need to form groups and groups' tendency to treat their members more favorably than they treat outsiders.

Display slide 8–11. Discuss questions on the slide. Ask participants to share their own experiences regarding informal social networks in the workplace. Emphasize that it is important for people to be aware of how their in-group biases influence their behavior at work. Explain that often we are not aware of how we treat people differently, depending on the perception that they belong to our group or do not belong.

10:10 Learning Activity 12–2: Seeking Connections (25 minutes)

10:35 Learning Activity 12–3: Personal Commitment (10 minutes)

10:45 Conclusion and evaluation (15 minutes)

Make your concluding remarks. Thank participants for their efforts in the training session. Distribute Assessment 13–2: Sample Level 1 Evaluation and ask everyone to complete the evaluation and place it on a table as they leave the room.

What to Do Next

- Gather materials to run this module with a small group of volunteers.
- Pilot-test the module and ask participants to give you feedback.
- Adjust the module according to the feedback you receive and the specific needs of your organization.
- Develop a process to encourage participants to share the commitments they have made with their supervisors or with a Conversity partner.

◆◆◆

Seeking Conversity means seeking common ground. It doesn't mean that differences do not exist. Human differences in culture often have a significant impact on communications. An engaging and dynamic module discussing cultural differences is thoroughly described in the following chapter.

Slide 8–1

Conversity Leadership

Module 1: Out of the Box

Cris Wildermuth, M.Ed.
Susan D. Gray, PHR

Slide 8–2

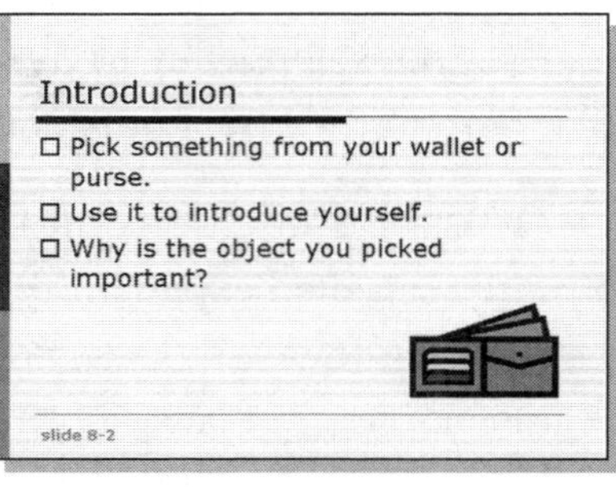

Introduction
☐ Pick something from your wallet or purse.
☐ Use it to introduce yourself.
☐ Why is the object you picked important?
slide 8-2

Slide 8–3

Agenda
☐ The P²C² Challenge
☐ Groups R Us
☐ Introducing Conversity
slide 8-3

Slide 8–4

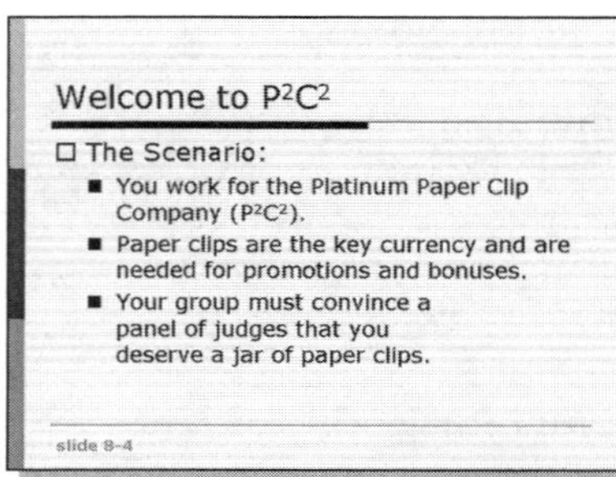

Welcome to P²C²
☐ The Scenario:
■ You work for the Platinum Paper Clip Company (P²C²).
■ Paper clips are the key currency and are needed for promotions and bonuses.
■ Your group must convince a panel of judges that you deserve a jar of paper clips.
slide 8-4

Slide 8–5

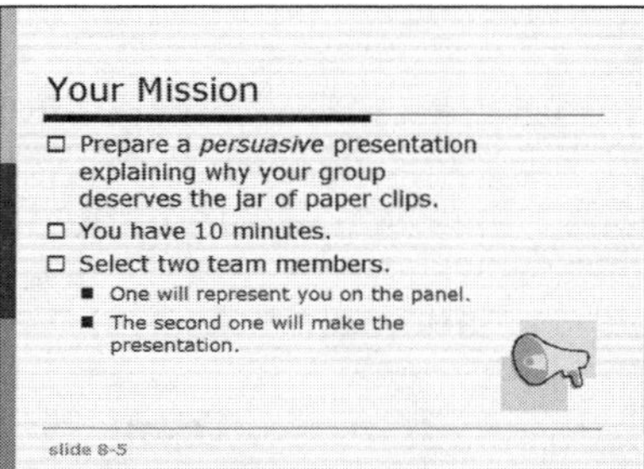

Your Mission
☐ Prepare a *persuasive* presentation explaining why your group deserves the jar of paper clips.
☐ You have 10 minutes.
☐ Select two team members.
■ One will represent you on the panel.
■ The second one will make the presentation.
slide 8-5

Slide 8–6

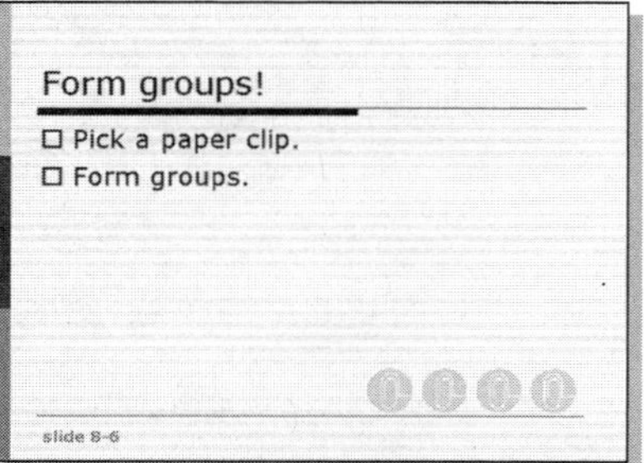

Form groups!
☐ Pick a paper clip.
☐ Form groups.
slide 8-6

Slide 8–7

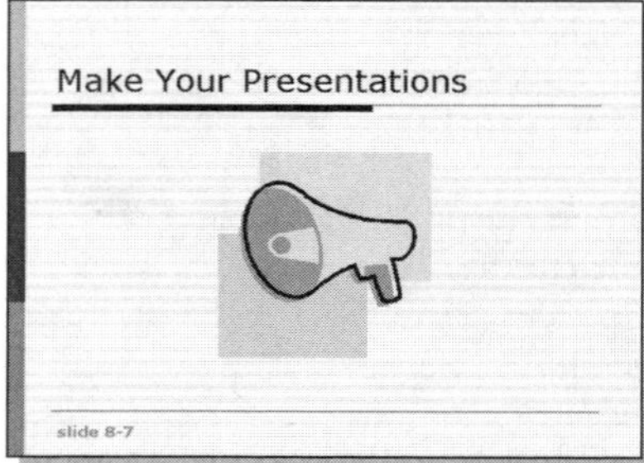

Slide 8–8

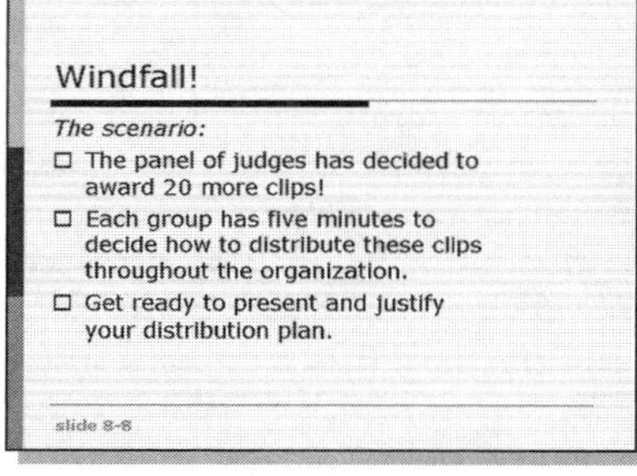

Windfall!
The scenario:
☐ The panel of judges has decided to award 20 more clips!
☐ Each group has five minutes to decide how to distribute these clips throughout the organization.
☐ Get ready to present and justify your distribution plan.
slide 8-8

Slide 8–9

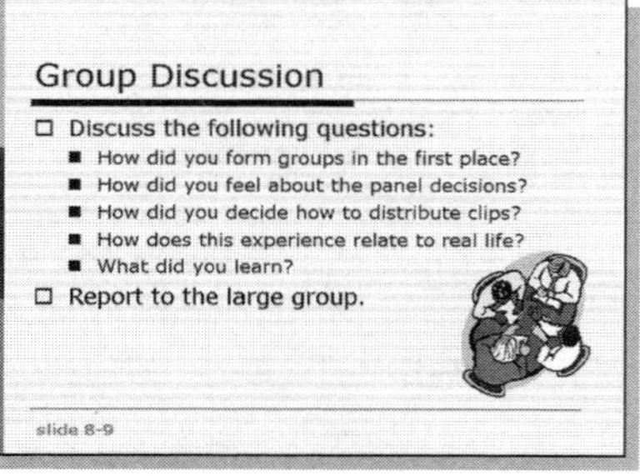

Group Discussion
☐ Discuss the following questions:
■ How did you form groups in the first place?
■ How did you feel about the panel decisions?
■ How did you decide how to distribute clips?
■ How does this experience relate to real life?
■ What did you learn?
☐ Report to the large group.
slide 8-9

Slide 8–10

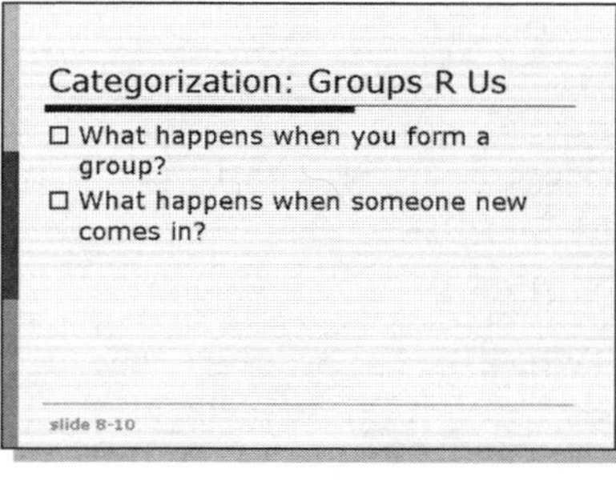

Categorization: Groups R Us
☐ What happens when you form a group?
☐ What happens when someone new comes in?
slide 8-10

Slide 8–11

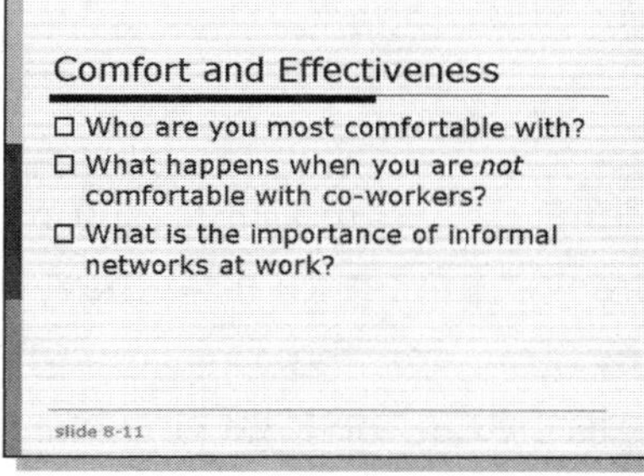

Comfort and Effectiveness
☐ Who are you most comfortable with?
☐ What happens when you are *not* comfortable with co-workers?
☐ What is the importance of informal networks at work?
slide 8-11

Slide 8–12

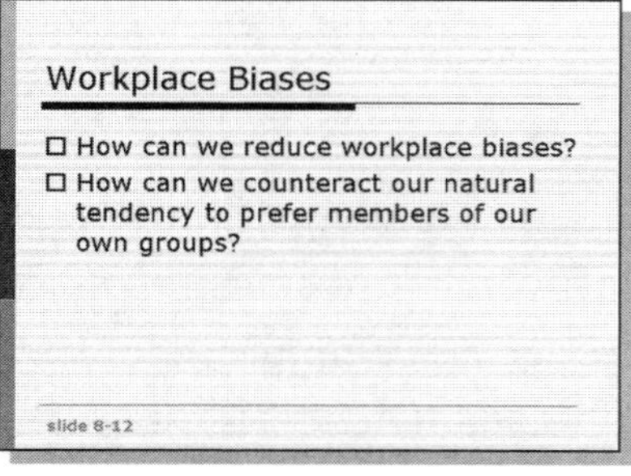

Workplace Biases
☐ How can we reduce workplace biases?
☐ How can we counteract our natural tendency to prefer members of our own groups?
slide 8-12

Slide 8–13

Conversity

Con: Latin for *with, together, for*
Verse: *To familiarize by experience, study, or practice*

slide 8-13

Slide 8–14

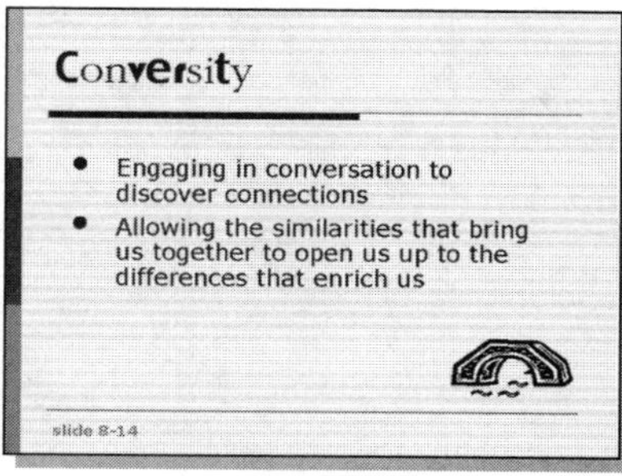

Conversity
• Engaging in conversation to discover connections
• Allowing the similarities that bring us together to open us up to the differences that enrich us
slide 8-14

Slide 8–15

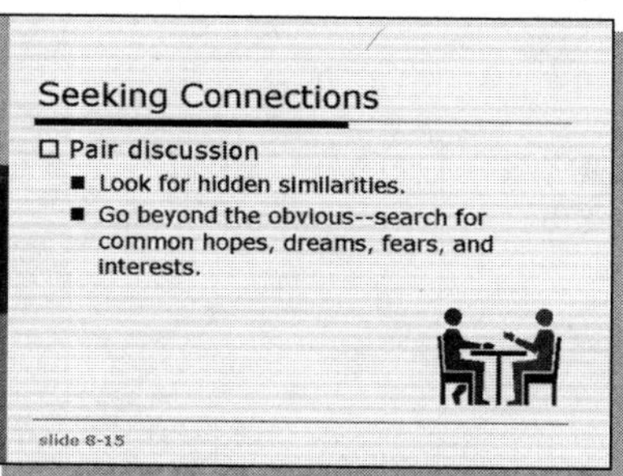

Seeking Connections
□ Pair discussion
■ Look for hidden similarities.
■ Go beyond the obvious--search for common hopes, dreams, fears, and interests.
slide 8-15

Slide 8–16

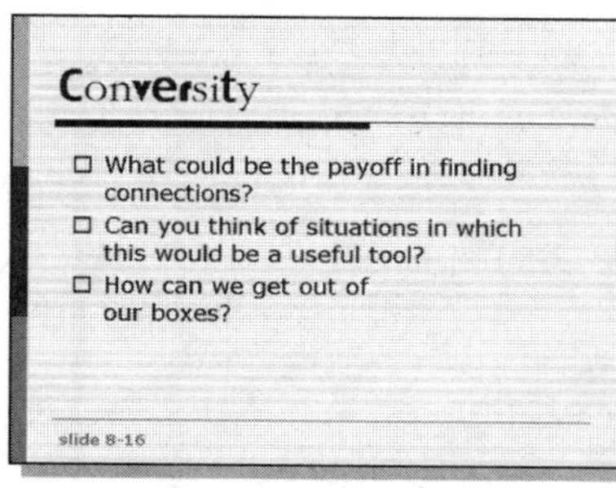

Conversity
□ What could be the payoff in finding connections?
□ Can you think of situations in which this would be a useful tool?
□ How can we get out of our boxes?
slide 8-16

Slide 8–17

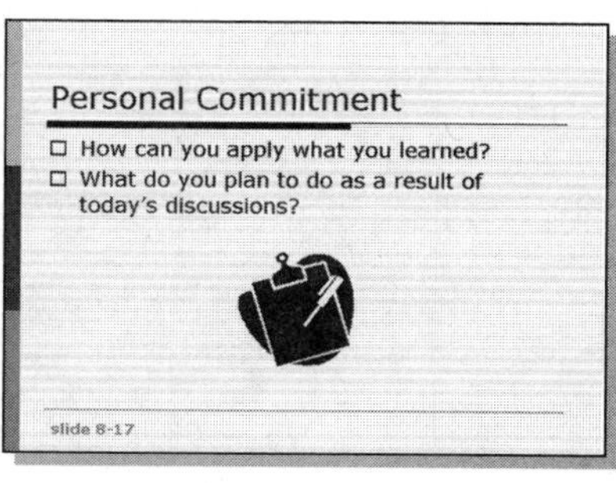

Personal Commitment
□ How can you apply what you learned?
□ What do you plan to do as a result of today's discussions?
slide 8-17

Chapter 9

Module 2: Cultures and Values

What's in This Chapter?

- Objectives for the four-hour module on cultural diversity
- Discussion of the legal safety of the instructional activities contained in the module
- List of materials for the facilitator and the participants
- Sample program agenda

When you travel, remember that a foreign country is not designed to make you comfortable. It is designed to make its own people comfortable.

– Clifton Fadiman (1904–1999), U.S. writer and radio host

In the first module you helped participants understand how important similarities are and why people often prefer to stick to their own groups. But it is important for participants eventually to become comfortable with the idea that people are not all similar. Conversity is a basis for growth, not the ultimate goal.

Module 2: Cultures and Values introduces participants to intercultural differences. Participants discuss their own cultural programming in various dimensions, such as communications, hierarchy, and equality. Next they have the opportunity to connect their cultures with deeply held values. Even though value differences cause significant problems in intercultural and interpersonal relationships at work, many diversity professionals are reluctant to address them. It is possible, however, to address values in a nonjudgmental way. The exercises in this module do not attempt to convince participants to adopt a specific set of values but simply to be respectful of value differences and sensitive to their impact on workplace decisions.

What Is Culture?

The word *culture* has multiple definitions. Dutch interculturalist Geert Hofstede (1997) defined culture as "the collective programming of the mind which distinguishes the members of one group or category of people from another" (p. 5). The culture of a group involves its ways of being and behaving, what it considers appropriate and inappropriate, and its values. The word *values*, used in this context, means "broad tendencies" (Hofstede, 1997, p. 8) or preferences for certain issues, behaviors, or situations over others. Typically someone's values have to do with what that person considers "most important." For instance, everyone may agree that family and money are important, but some people prioritize money over family and others prioritize family over money.

For additional information on the subjects covered in this module, a useful and easy-to-read resource is the book *Survival Kit for Multicultural Living,* by Ellen Summerfield. A good way to extend the value of this session is to have a copy of this book available for each participant and ask them to read it and then report on it at a future meeting.

This chapter includes complete instructions for conducting a training with this module. You will need about four hours to complete it.

All instructions included in this module assume you will have a group of 20 participants, subdivided into four small groups of 5 members. If your group size is different, please adjust the quantities of materials accordingly.

If you plan to present more modules after this one, make sure participants know how to register for them. It is useful to run all modules with the same group and the same facilitator(s) so that trust and comfort levels within the class gradually improve.

How Safe Is Module 2?

People tend to find cultural differences intriguing and they typically are willing to explore them without much encouragement. The cultural differences portion of this module is unlikely to generate much resistance and so is relatively safe. Value issues, however, may generate some heated discussions that must be skillfully facilitated.

Training Objectives

The objectives for Module 2 are to help participants

- describe human cultures and their impact on human assumptions, values, beliefs, rituals, and behaviors
- examine their own cultural assumptions, values, beliefs, rituals, and behaviors
- choose nonjudgmental language when discussing issues that may be influenced by people's cultures and value systems.

Materials

There are several things you will need to facilitate this presentation. The list below will help you prepare properly.

For the instructor:

- Learning Activity 12–3: Personal Commitment
- Learning Activity 12–4: The Interview
- Learning Activity 12–5: Your Cultural Continuum
- Learning Activity 12–6: Values Line
- Learning Activity 12–7: Value Congruency
- Learning Activity 12–8: Value Decision Making
- Learning Activity 12–9: Figuring Things Out
- Tool 13–2: Cultural Rules Card Set
- Tool 13–3: Values Card Set
- Projector, screen, and computer for running the PowerPoint presentation
- PowerPoint slides 9–1 through 9–26 (*Module 2.ppt* on the CD; thumbnail copies of the slides appear at the end of this chapter)
- Flipchart and marking pen

For the participants:

- Assessment 13–2: Sample Level 1 Evaluation

- Tool 13–1: Interviewer Questions
- Training Instrument 13–6: Personal Commitment Worksheet
- Training Instrument 13–7: Group Brainstorm
- Training Instrument 13–8: The Interview
- Training Instrument 13–9: Your Cultural Continuum
- Training Instrument 13–10: Value Congruency
- Training Instrument 13–11: Value Decision Making
- Training Instrument 13–12: Figuring Things Out
- Flipchart, marking pens, magazines, scissors, glue (optional)
- Some play money (optional)

Using the CD

Materials for this training session are provided in this workbook and as electronic files on the accompanying CD. To access the electronic files, insert the CD and click on the appropriate Adobe .pdf or PowerPoint .ppt/.pps files. Further directions and help using the files can be found in the appendix, "Using the Compact Disc," at the back of this workbook.

It's important that you review all of the slides as part of your preparation for the workshop. At that time you should plan explanations and examples for concepts presented in the slides.

As with all the other materials in this book, you may adapt the slides and handouts as long as you include in all your presentation materials the authors' names, company name, the title of this book, and copyright information.

Module 2 Sample Agenda

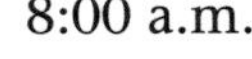

8:00 a.m. Welcome (5 minutes)

Display slide 9–1. Welcome participants and thank them for taking part in the session.

Note: We are assuming that the people participating in this session are those who participated in Module 1, so no icebreaker or time for introductions is needed. If the group includes new participants, make sure to reserve some time for introductions. One possible introductory icebreaker exercise is to ask each participant to reveal one interesting fact about his or her background and experience that few people in the room know.

8:05 Review of Module 1 (10 minutes)

Display slide 9–2. Distribute Training Instrument 13–7 to participants and ask each group to use the questions there as a guide for a recap of the most important points covered in Module 1. Debrief discussions with the large group. Remind people that Conversity—finding common ground—should be a general theme for all diversity initiatives at the organization.

Creative alternative: Provide participants with a flipchart, marking pens, and other materials (magazines, glue, scissors) and ask them to make a poster that illustrates the key lesson from Module 1.

8:15 Present the agenda (5 minutes)

Display slide 9–3. Explain that having focused in Module 1 on similarities, it is time to deal with the significant differences among human beings. Tell participants that among these differences are cultural background and the value systems that cultures develop and enforce. Explain that culture will be the main focus of today's discussions. During the program they will take part in a cultural simulation, define culture and its impact on human relationships, and have a special discussion on cultural values. Add that participants will have the opportunity to look at problems from other people's perspectives in the final exercise.

8:20 Learning Activity 12–4: The Interview (40 minutes)

9:00 Brief lecture on cultural dimensions (10 minutes)

Display slide 9–7. Explain that cultures differ in some major areas called "cultural dimensions," and that these dimensions have been studied extensively.

Display slide 9–8. Explain that even though most people readily identify visible aspects of culture (for example, art and music, architecture, clothing, and celebrations), the invisible aspects of culture include the dimensions that most often cause misunderstandings between people. Display slide 9–9 and describe the fundamental and less apparent cultural dimensions that differentiate human cultures:

- **Communication style:** In some cultures, people prefer a very direct style, saying exactly what they mean; in others, people prefer to be more indirect and to speak between the lines.
- **Need for harmony:** In certain cultures, conflict is highly undesirable; in others, harmony is the utmost goal.
- **Sense of time:** Exact time is an absolute priority in some cultures, but not everywhere in the world.
- **Gender equality:** Gender roles are very rigidly divided in some cultures; in others, men and women may perform the same roles and behave similarly without negative consequences.
- **Hierarchy:** For some cultures, hierarchy is a way to bring order to chaos and is accepted by all members of society; in other cultures, equality is the expressed societal goal.
- **Relationships:** In some cultures it is vital to build relationships to obtain success in all areas of life, including business negotiations; other cultures value individual efforts and independence.

Two Key Points:

1. You will want to reinforce the fact that cultural dimensions exist along a continuum and that cultures place themselves somewhere along that scale of intensity. Individuals, however, may differ from the norms of their cultures.

2. Participants may ask, "What is the difference between cultural dimensions and stereotypes?" Explain that although contrasts in cultural dimensions have been identified through a great amount of research, *any* generalization (even those based on research findings) has the potential to become a stereotype. A stereotype can be defined as a *fixed* generalization.

9:10 Learning Activity 12–5: Your Cultural Continuum (35 minutes)

9:45 Break (15 minutes)

10:00 Learning Activity 12–6: Values Line (10 minutes)

10:10 Learning Activity 12–7: Value Congruency (45 minutes)

10:55 Learning Activity 12–8: Value Decision Making (25 minutes)

11:20 Learning Activity 12–9: Figuring Things Out (25 minutes)

Time-saving alternative: If you are running out of time, cut this exercise or reserve it for a follow-up session.

11:45 Learning Activity 12–3: Personal Commitment (10 minutes)

Display slide 9–26. Distribute copies of Training Instrument 13–6: Personal Commitment Worksheet. Ask participants to complete their worksheets individually.

11:55 Conclusion and evaluation (10 minutes)

Make your concluding remarks. If an additional session is scheduled, make sure participants know how to sign up for it. Thank participants for their efforts in the training session. Distribute a copy of Assessment 13–2: Sample Level 1 Evaluation to each person. Ask them to complete the evaluation and place it on a table as they leave the room.

What to Do Next

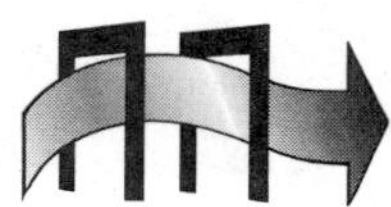

- Read *Survival Kit for Multicultural Living* (Summerfield, 1997).
- Gather materials to run this module with a small group of volunteers.

- Pilot-test the module and ask participants to give you feedback.
- Adjust the module according to the feedback you receive and the specific needs of your organization.
- Develop a process to encourage participants to share the commitments they have made with their supervisors or with a Conversity partner.

◆◆◆

It is common for organizations to address their diversity issues in a legalistic and policy-driven way: Employees are introduced to harassment workshops and sign their agreement with antidiscrimination policies. Although these activities may be recommended for legal reasons, they are unlikely to significantly improve diversity relations. A list of detailed policies in an employee manual probably won't make your employees help each other reach their fullest potential and celebrate one another's achievements.

The following two chapters help solve this problem by addressing two highly sensitive topics in diversity relations: stereotypes and prejudiced attitudes. These topics were placed in Modules 3 and 4 intentionally. It is important for participants to be comfortable with one another and with the instructor before they can open up and discuss deeply held attitudes toward people who are different from them. Chapter 10 gives complete instructions on running Module 3: First Impressions (stereotypes) and chapter 11 presents Module 4: Walking in Their Shoes (understanding prejudice).

Slide 9–1

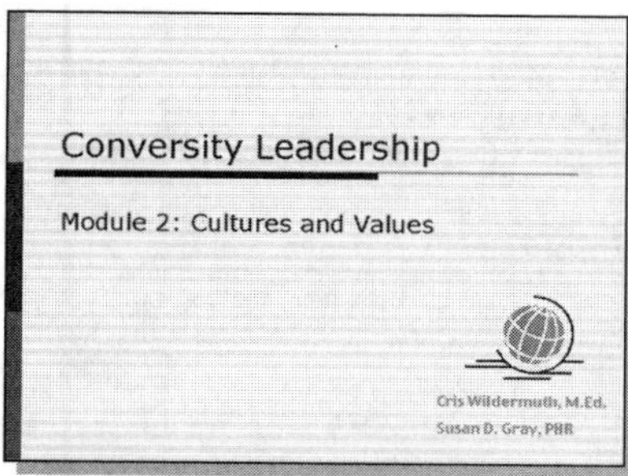

Slide 9–2

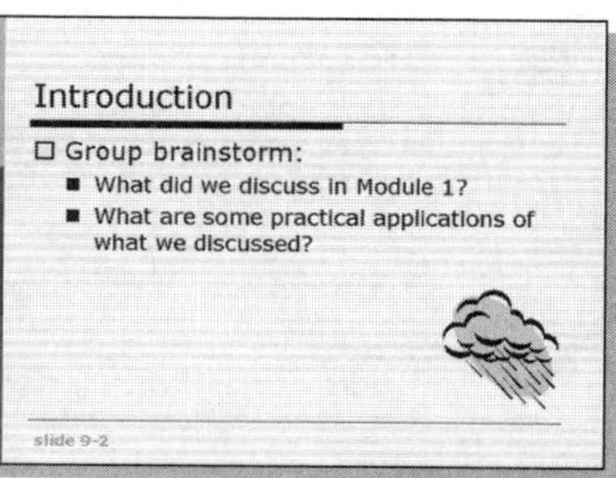

Introduction
☐ Group brainstorm:
■ What did we discuss in Module 1?
■ What are some practical applications of what we discussed?
slide 9-2

Slide 9–3

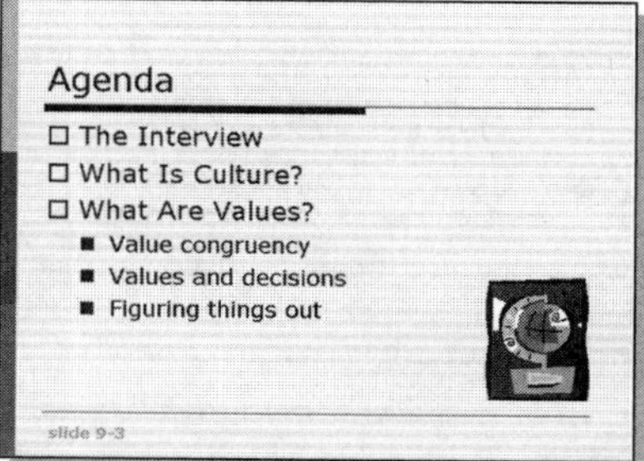

Slide 9–4

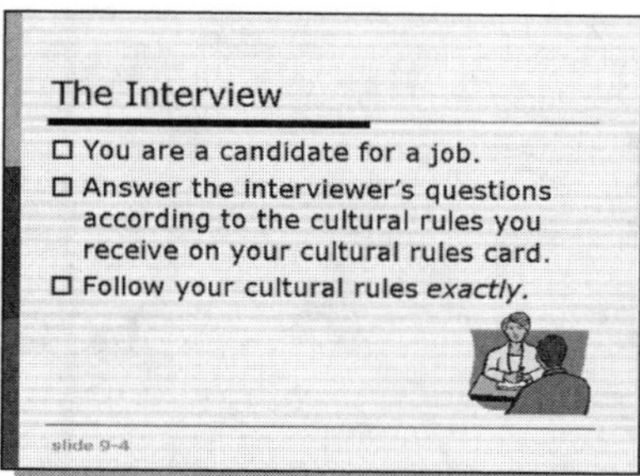

The Interview
☐ You are a candidate for a job.
☐ Answer the interviewer's questions according to the cultural rules you receive on your cultural rules card.
☐ Follow your cultural rules exactly.
slide 9-4

Slide 9–5

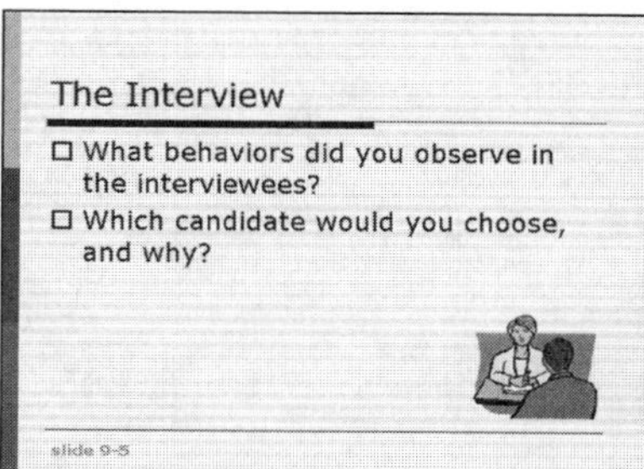

The Interview
☐ What behaviors did you observe in the interviewees?
☐ Which candidate would you choose, and why?
slide 9-5

Slide 9–6

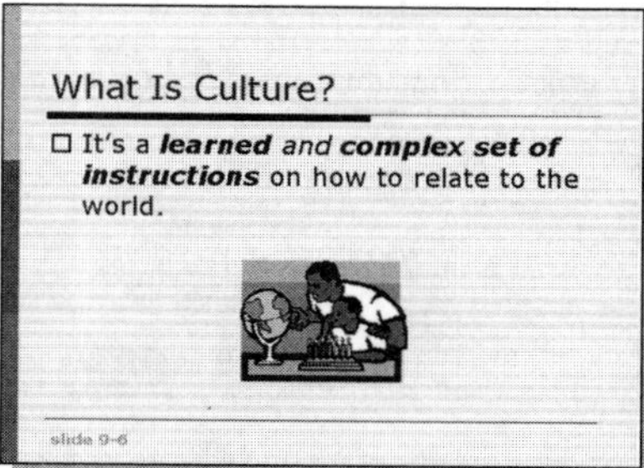

What Is Culture?
☐ It's a learned and complex set of instructions on how to relate to the world.
slide 9-6

Slide 9–7

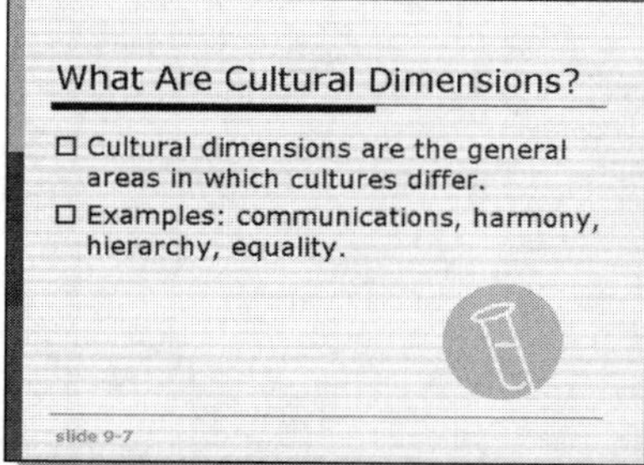

What Are Cultural Dimensions?
☐ Cultural dimensions are the general areas in which cultures differ.
☐ Examples: communications, harmony, hierarchy, equality.
slide 9-7

Slide 9–8

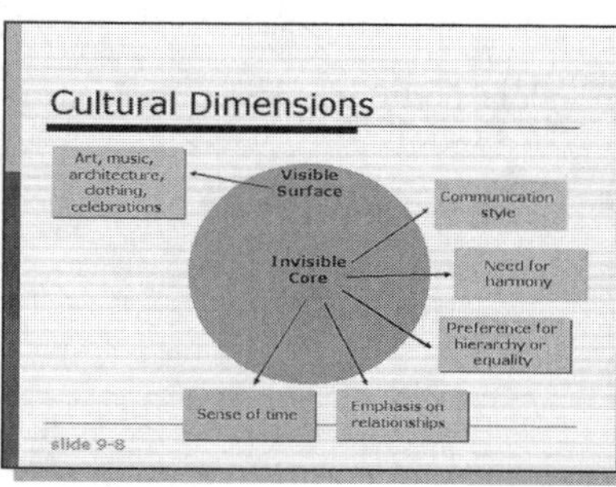

Slide 9–9

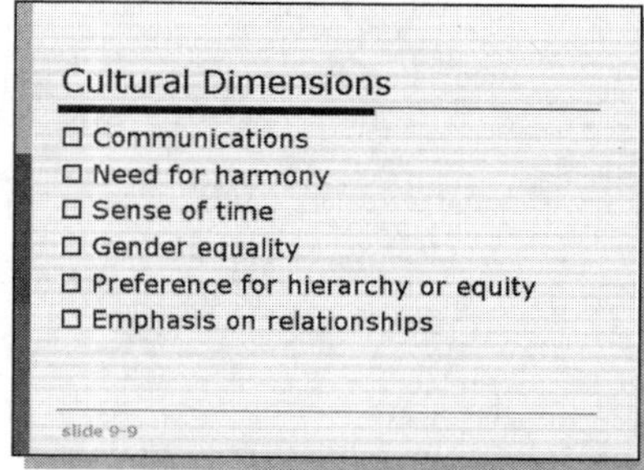

Cultural Dimensions
☐ Communications
☐ Need for harmony
☐ Sense of time
☐ Gender equality
☐ Preference for hierarchy or equity
☐ Emphasis on relationships
slide 9-9

Slide 9–10

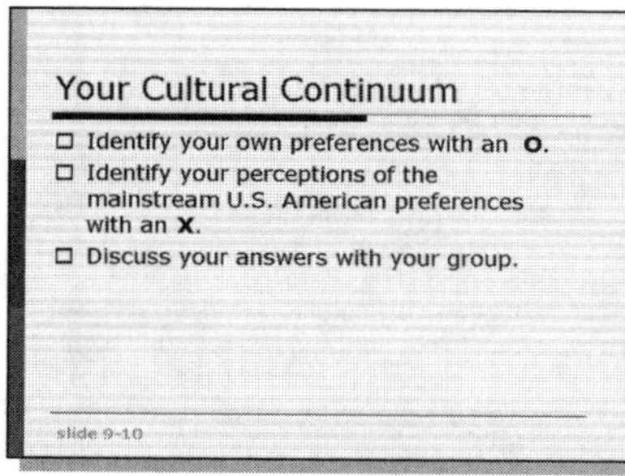

Your Cultural Continuum
☐ Identify your own preferences with an O.
☐ Identify your perceptions of the mainstream U.S. American preferences with an X.
☐ Discuss your answers with your group.
slide 9-10

Slide 9–11

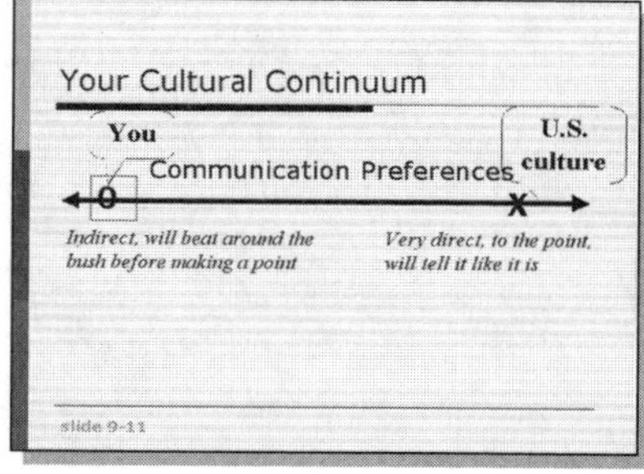

Slide 9–12

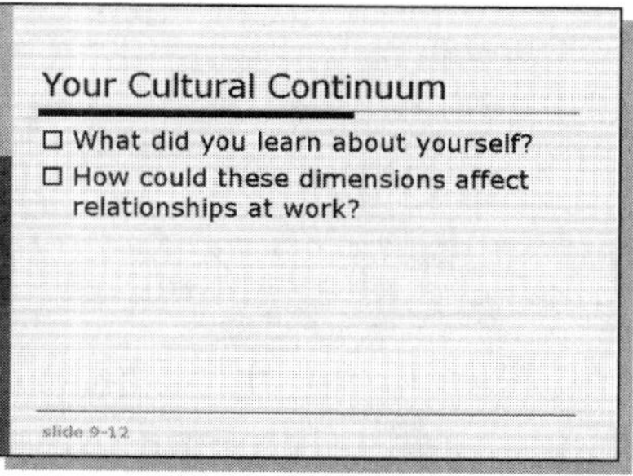

Your Cultural Continuum
☐ What did you learn about yourself?
☐ How could these dimensions affect relationships at work?
slide 9-12

Slide 9–13

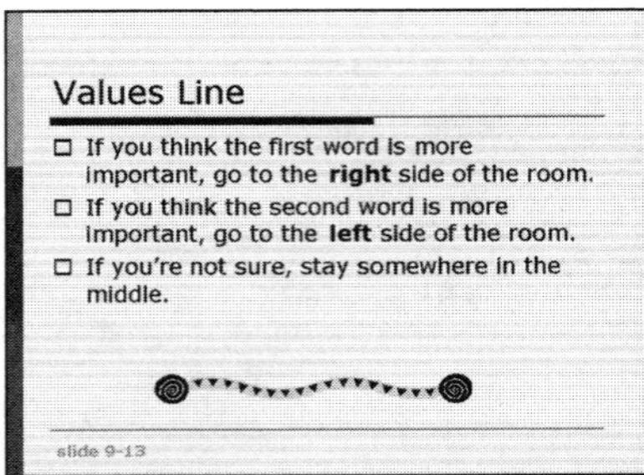

Values Line
☐ If you think the first word is more important, go to the **right** side of the room.
☐ If you think the second word is more important, go to the **left** side of the room.
☐ If you're not sure, stay somewhere in the middle.
slide 9-13

Slide 9–14

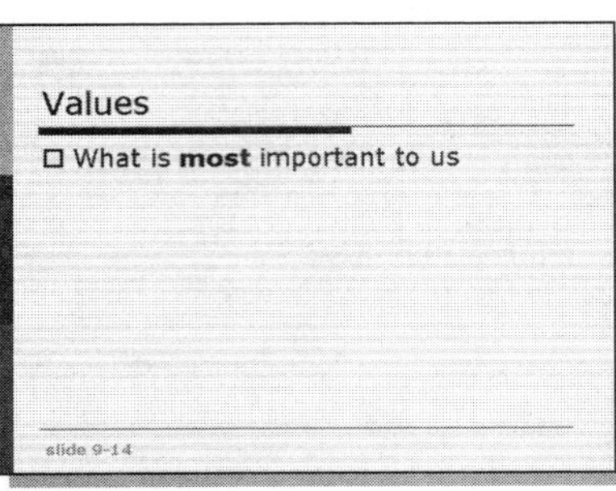

Values
☐ What is **most** important to us
slide 9-14

Slide 9–15

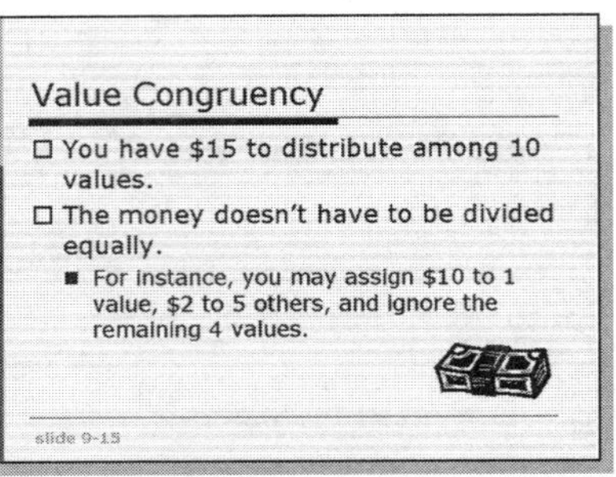

Value Congruency
☐ You have $15 to distribute among 10 values.
☐ The money doesn't have to be divided equally.
■ For instance, you may assign $10 to 1 value, $2 to 5 others, and ignore the remaining 4 values.
slide 9-15

Slide 9–16

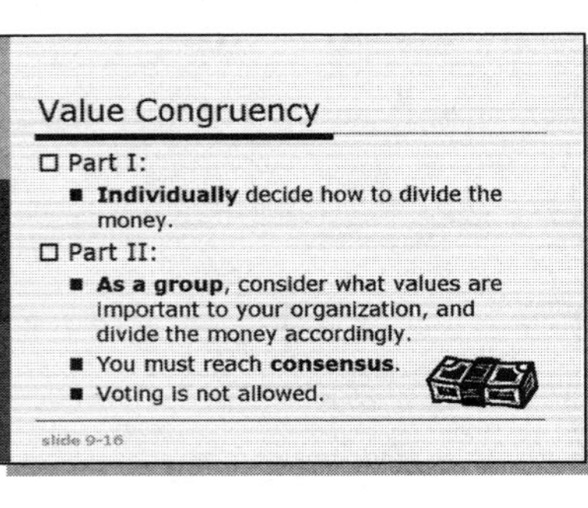

Value Congruency
☐ Part I:
■ **Individually** decide how to divide the money.
☐ Part II:
■ **As a group**, consider what values are important to your organization, and divide the money accordingly.
■ You must reach **consensus**.
■ Voting is not allowed.
slide 9-16

Slide 9–17

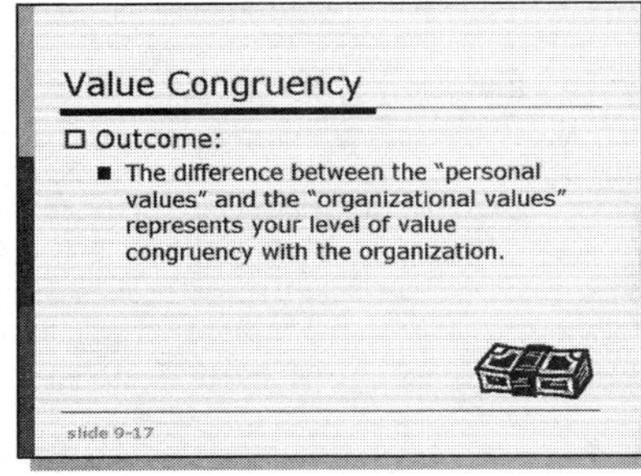

Value Congruency
☐ Outcome:
■ The difference between the "personal values" and the "organizational values" represents your level of value congruency with the organization.
slide 9-17

Slide 9–18

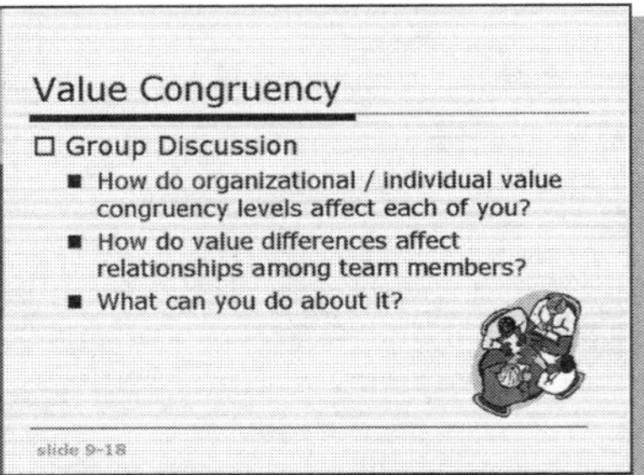

Value Congruency
☐ Group Discussion
■ How do organizational / individual value congruency levels affect each of you?
■ How do value differences affect relationships among team members?
■ What can you do about it?
slide 9-18

Slide 9–19

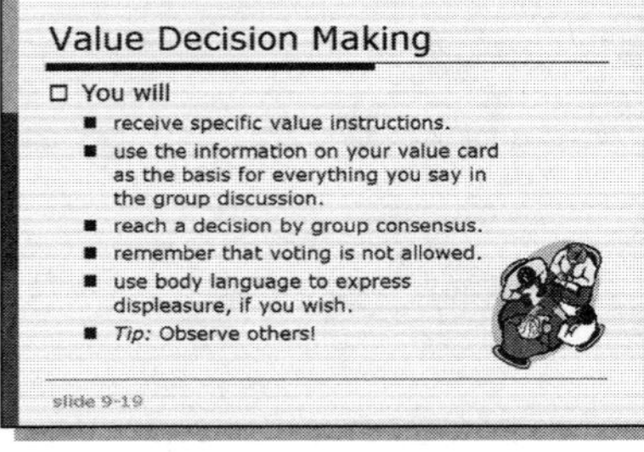

Value Decision Making
☐ You will
■ receive specific value instructions.
■ use the information on your value card as the basis for everything you say in the group discussion.
■ reach a decision by group consensus.
■ remember that voting is not allowed.
■ use body language to express displeasure, if you wish.
■ *Tip:* Observe others!
slide 9-19

Slide 9–20

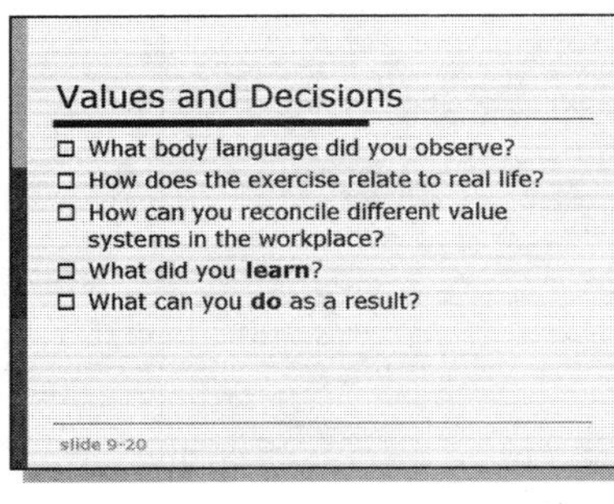

Values and Decisions
☐ What body language did you observe?
☐ How does the exercise relate to real life?
☐ How can you reconcile different value systems in the workplace?
☐ What did you **learn**?
☐ What can you **do** as a result?
slide 9-20

Slide 9–21

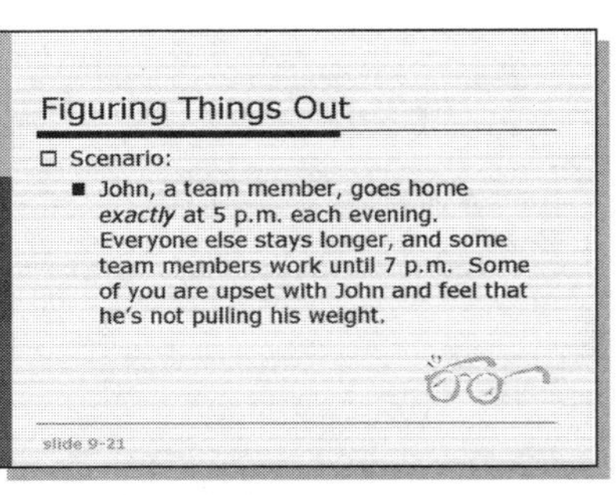

Figuring Things Out
☐ Scenario:
■ John, a team member, goes home *exactly* at 5 p.m. each evening. Everyone else stays longer, and some team members work until 7 p.m. Some of you are upset with John and feel that he's not pulling his weight.
slide 9-21

Slide 9–22

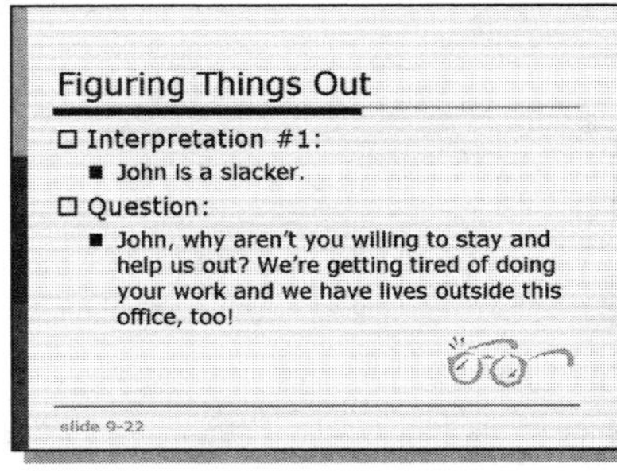

Figuring Things Out
☐ Interpretation #1:
■ John is a slacker.
☐ Question:
■ John, why aren't you willing to stay and help us out? We're getting tired of doing your work and we have lives outside this office, too!
slide 9-22

Slide 9–23

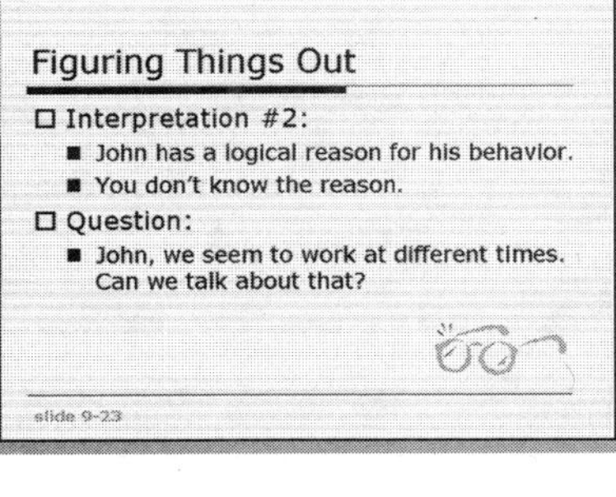

Figuring Things Out
☐ Interpretation #2:
■ John has a logical reason for his behavior.
■ You don't know the reason.
☐ Question:
■ John, we seem to work at different times. Can we talk about that?
slide 9-23

Slide 9–24

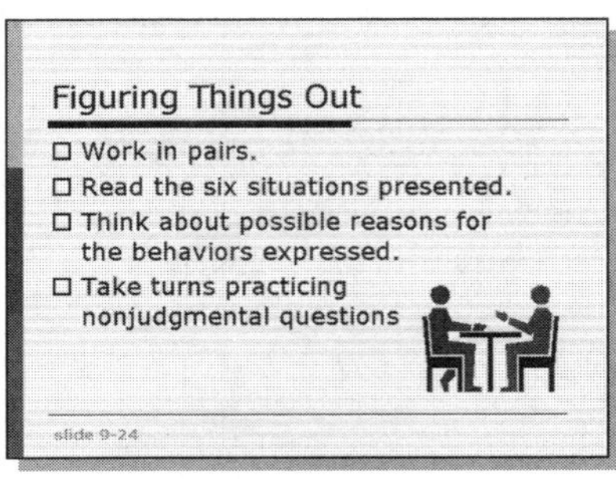

Figuring Things Out
☐ Work in pairs.
☐ Read the six situations presented.
☐ Think about possible reasons for the behaviors expressed.
☐ Take turns practicing nonjudgmental questions
slide 9-24

Slide 9–25

Figuring Things Out

- What could be the payoff?
- Can you think of situations in which this would be a useful tool?
- How can you use Conversity to conciliate differences in values?

slide 9-25

Slide 9–26

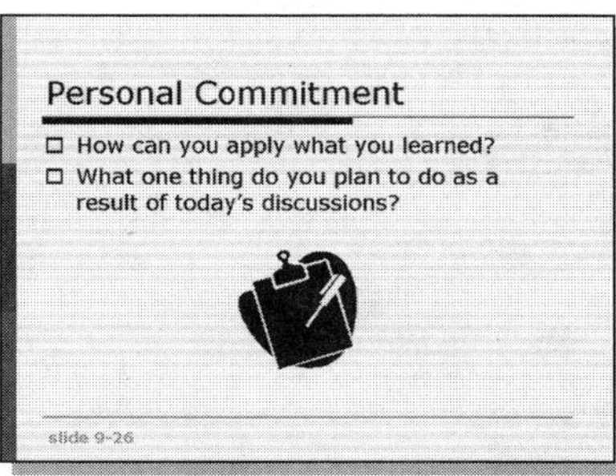

Personal Commitment
How can you apply what you learned?
What one thing do you plan to do as a result of today's discussions?
slide 9-26

Chapter 10

Module 3: First Impressions

What's in This Chapter?

- Objectives for the three-hour module on stereotypes
- Discussion of the legal safety of the instructional activities contained in the module
- List of materials for the facilitator and the participants
- Sample program agenda

Common sense is the collection of prejudices acquired by age eighteen.
– Attributed to Albert Einstein (1879–1955),
physicist and genius

In the last module you helped participants appreciate the importance of culture and the impact of different value systems in the workplace.

Module 3: First Impressions and Module 4: Walking in Their Shoes address two key diversity topics: stereotypes and prejudices. You are now reaching a core piece in your diversity initiative—and a sensitive one. If you did your groundwork by completing Modules 1 and 2, participants should be ready to start addressing the root of discriminatory behaviors, whether subtle or overt.

The goal of Module 3 is not to eliminate stereotypes altogether—that's an impossible task because stereotypes are natural cognitive responses, ways of organizing the huge volumes of information humans receive daily. The overall goal of this module is to generate an awareness of stereotypes and prevent stereotype rigidity. Such rigidity is a person's inability to change a stereotype even when confronted with evidence that disproves it.

This chapter includes complete instructions for conducting a training with this module. You should spend 2.5 to 3 hours presenting it.

All instructions included in this module assume you will have a class of 20 participants, subdivided into four small groups of 5 members. If your group size is different, please adjust the quantities of materials accordingly.

How Safe Is Module 3?

The activities contained in this module focus mostly on attitudes. Designing interventions that can potentially influence attitudes is very challenging because attitudes take a long time to develop and are, by definition, hidden from view.

Facilitating attitude development sessions can be tricky. It is a good idea to have your less experienced facilitators observe the old-timers in action before they try these efforts on their own.

Some organizations are strongly against addressing attitudes in workplace training, especially when the training is mandatory. The problem is that you are unlikely to affect discriminatory behaviors without addressing the prejudiced attitudes behind them. Ultimately, however, you will need to make your own decision based on the climate at your organization, the amount of time you have for a diversity intervention, and guidance from your legal counsel.

If you do choose to run this module, make sure that participants are prepared by having completed Modules 1 and 2. It is ideal to have the same participants and the same facilitator(s) throughout the entire diversity sequence. This way the participants' comfort levels with one another and with the facilitator are likely to increase with each module. By the time the more challenging modules are reached, participants are more likely to be ready and willing to participate.

Training Objectives

The objectives for Module 3 are to help participants

- become aware of their own stereotypes
- discuss the origin of stereotypes and their impact on decision making
- be willing and able to question stereotypes and discard old ones when new and disproving information is introduced.

Materials

There are several things you will need to facilitate this presentation. The list below will help you prepare properly.

For the instructor:

- Learning Activity 12–3: Personal Commitment
- Learning Activity 12–10: Driver Portraits
- Learning Activity 12–11: Disproving Stereotypes
- Tool 13–4: Vehicle Card Set
- Projector, screen, and computer for running the PowerPoint presentation
- PowerPoint slides 10–1 through 10–14 (*Module 3.ppt* on the CD; thumbnail copies of the slides appear at the end of this chapter)
- Flipchart and marking pen

For the participants:

- Assessment 13–2: Sample Level 1 Evaluation
- Tool 13–5: Vehicle Card Composite Set
- Training Instrument 13–6: Personal Commitment Worksheet
- Training Instrument 13–7: Group Brainstorm
- Training Instrument 13–13: Driver Portraits
- Training Instrument 13–14: Disproving Stereotypes

Using the CD

Materials for this training session are provided in this workbook and as electronic files on the accompanying CD. To access the electronic files, insert the CD and click on the appropriate Adobe .pdf or PowerPoint .ppt/.pps files. Further directions and help using the files can be found in the appendix, "Using the Compact Disc," at the back of this workbook.

It's important that you review all of the slides as part of your preparation for the workshop. At that time you should plan explanations and examples for concepts presented in the slides.

As with all the other materials in this book, you may adapt the slides and handouts as long as you include in all your presentation materials the authors' names, company name, the title of this book, and the copyright information.

Module 3 Sample Agenda

8:00 a.m. Welcome (5 minutes)

Display slide 10–1. Welcome participants and thank them for taking part in the session.

8:05 Review of Module 1 (10 minutes)

Display slide 10–2. Distribute a copy of Training Instrument 13–7 to each participant. Ask each group to use the questions on Training Instrument 13–7 as a guide for a recap of the most important points presented in Module 2. Debrief discussions with the large group. Remind people that Conversity—finding common ground—should be a general theme for all diversity initiatives at the organization.

8:15 Introductions: The best things in life (10 minutes)

Display slide 10–3. Ask participants to think of a way to complete the sentence on the slide using one or a few words. You may choose to write an example on the flipchart, such as "The best things in life are achieved through teamwork." Have participants complete the sentence aloud, one at a time. If participants don't know one another, this is a good opportunity to break the ice. Ask them to complete the sentence and say who they are, where they work, and so forth.

Tip: Have a volunteer write on the flipchart some of the words and phrases used to complete the sentence. Use those sentences later to create a motivational poster for distribution in your organization.

Time-saving alternative: Let the introductions and sentence completion activity take place in small groups. Ask for a volunteer in each group to capture the sentences for later use in a motivational poster.

8:25 Present the agenda (5 minutes)

Display slide 10–4. Briefly explain that participants will engage in an exercise involving cars and drivers before they begin to discuss the central topic of the session—first impressions.

Tip: It is best to go very briefly through the agenda. Avoid emphasizing a discussion of stereotypes before the Driver Portraits exercise. Otherwise, participants may be reluctant to participate freely.

8:30 Learning Activity 12–10: Driver Portraits (35 minutes)

9:05 Break (10 minutes)

9:15 Brief lecture on stereotypes (20 minutes)

Note: Throughout this lecture, ask participants for examples and for their active participation in making the content *real* for them. Most people can't sustain interest in a lecture for more than 10 minutes unless the lecture is interspersed with short discussions.

Display slide 10–7. Read or paraphrase the contents of the slide. Explain that because we are continually bombarded with information, it is normal to make generalizations. A problem arises when a generalization becomes fixed and we refuse to change it, even when we receive information that disproves it.

Display slide 10–8. Explain that *priming* means the awakening of stereotypes. This awakening happens when we read about a news event or someone tells us stories about specific groups of people. Acknowledge that even the exercise participants just completed could remind them of stereotypes. Explain that priming is not an isolated or necessarily devious act; it occurs all the time. What is important is that people are aware of priming and learn to consciously change the stereotypes awakened by media reports or by comments made by others.

Display slide 10–9. Read or paraphrase the contents of the slide. Explain that stereotypes fulfill certain functions:

- They organize information by gathering people into certain categories (grouping).
- They reinforce group identification (social identity).
- They separate you from what happens to others (social detachment).
- They may even help raise one's self-esteem.

Note: The detachment function of stereotypes is interesting. Human conditions in society are differentiated, with some people having more advantages and privileges than others have. To make sense of this dissonance, humans commonly differentiate themselves from those in less privileged circumstances (that is, one may say, "They are poorer than me because they are lazy"). This is a normal human reaction that seeks to alleviate feelings of guilt and protect a person's self-esteem.

Display slide 10–10. Explain that stereotypes are normal and to be expected. The problem that people must address is not stereotype *formation,* but stereotype *rigidity.* Stereotype rigidity is the inability to change a stereotype even when a person receives disproving information.

Explain that because stereotypes are often subconscious, it is impossible to avoid them. What's important is to become aware of their existence.

Display slide 10–11. Summarize the discussion on stereotypes held so far by reading or paraphrasing the content of the slide.

Time-saving alternative: Reduce the information given to the group on stereotype formation, priming, and functions of stereotypes. Make sure to cover the information on rigidity—this is a very important and potentially damaging trait.

9:35 Small-group discussion (10 minutes)

Display slide 10–12 and refer participants to the group discussion questions in Training Instrument 13–13. Di-

rect each small group to choose a facilitator who will record the group's responses and report to the large group during the debriefing. Tell them they will have 10 minutes to discuss and answer the three questions.

9:45 Debrief the experience (10 minutes)

Have the facilitator in each small group present its findings.

Note: There are no right or wrong answers to any of the questions. Here's a possible answer to the question about Conversity techniques: *Through Conversity, people realize that they have a lot more in common than previously imagined. When commonalities are established, it becomes easier to get to know people better and thus disprove previously held stereotypes.*

9:55 Learning Activity 12–11: Disproving Stereotypes (25 minutes)

10:20 Learning Activity 12–3: Personal Commitment (10 minutes)

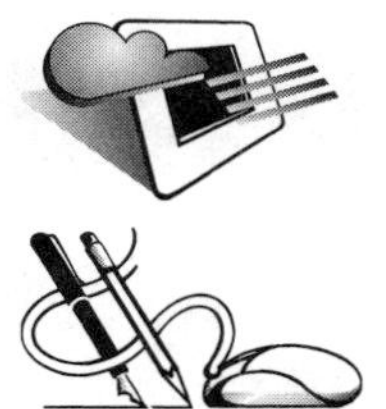

Display slide 10–14. Distribute a copy of Training Instrument 13–6 to each participant. Ask everyone to complete the worksheet individually.

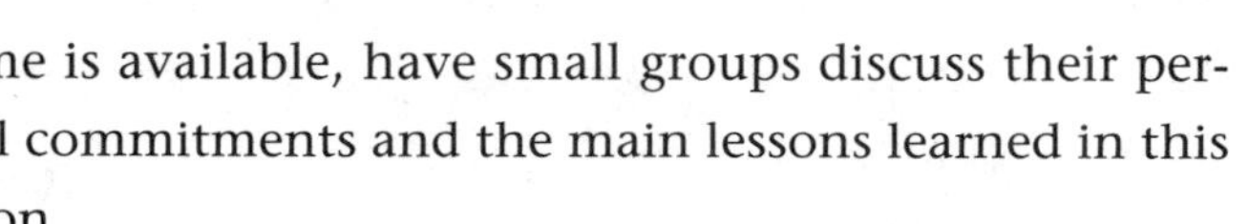

If time is available, have small groups discuss their personal commitments and the main lessons learned in this session.

10:30 Conclusion and evaluation (10 minutes)

Make your concluding remarks. If an additional session is scheduled, make sure participants know how to sign up for it. Thank participants for their efforts in the training session. Distribute a copy of Assessment 13–2: Sample Level 1 Evaluation to each person. Ask them to complete the evaluation and place it on a table as they leave the room.

What to Do Next

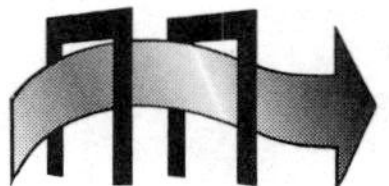

- Gather materials to run this module with a small group of volunteers.
- Pilot-test the module and ask participants to give you feedback.

- Adjust the module according to the feedback you receive and the specific needs of your organization.
- Develop a process to encourage participants to share the commitments they have made with their supervisors or with a Conversity partner.
- Set up small-group review sessions after you run this module. Participants will be able to review what they learned and discuss how they are applying that learning in the work environment. Remember that stereotypes take generations to form and they won't be dismantled in three hours, no matter how eye-opening your session.

◆◆◆

Understanding the origin of prejudices is an important step to improving diversity relationships. The next and vital step is for participants to learn to connect their unconscious prejudices with actual discriminatory behaviors. Because modern discrimination is often subtle it is easy for people to deny that it exists. The following chapter gives thorough instructions on how to run Module 4: Walking in Their Shoes, which helps participants connect their personal experiences related to prejudices with actual workplace behaviors. It is a powerful module that could have a significant impact on your diversity development initiative.

Slide 10–1

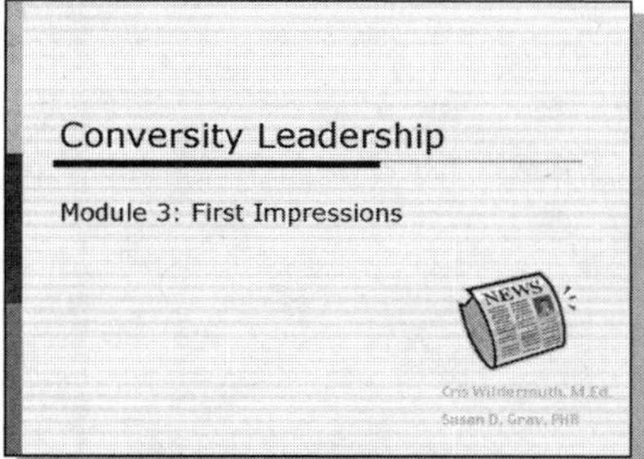

Conversity Leadership
Module 3: First Impressions
Cris Wildermuth, M.Ed.
Susan D. Gray, PhD

Slide 10–2

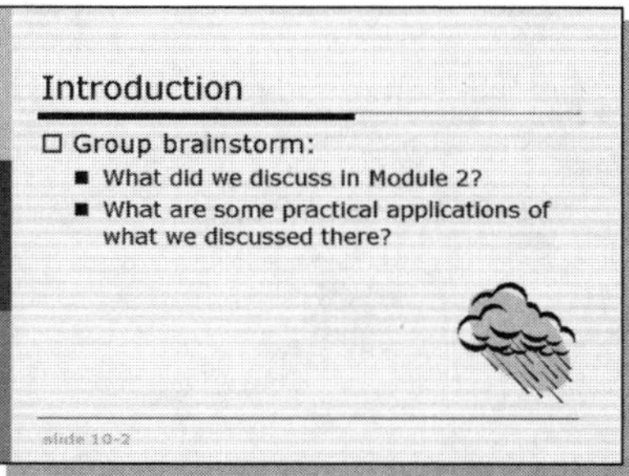

Introduction
☐ Group brainstorm:
■ What did we discuss in Module 2?
■ What are some practical applications of what we discussed there?
slide 10-2

Slide 10–3

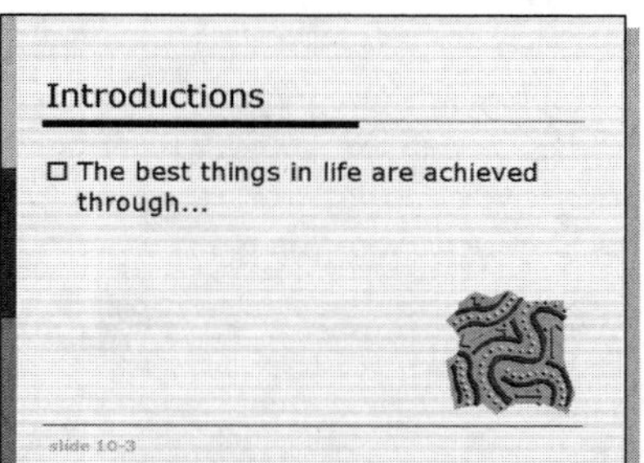

Introductions
☐ The best things in life are achieved through...
slide 10-3

Slide 10–4

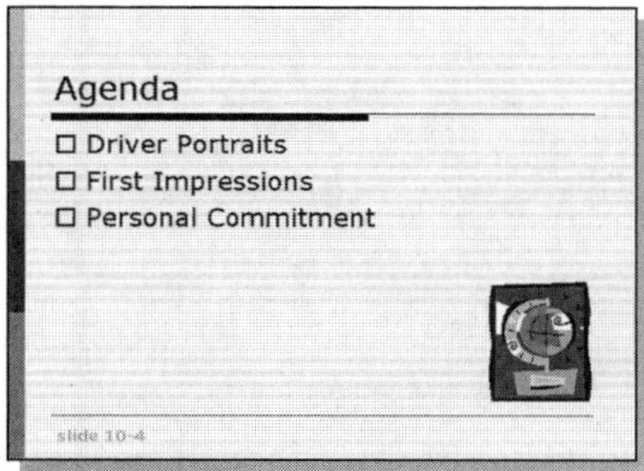

Agenda
☐ Driver Portraits
☐ First Impressions
☐ Personal Commitment
slide 10-4

Slide 10–5

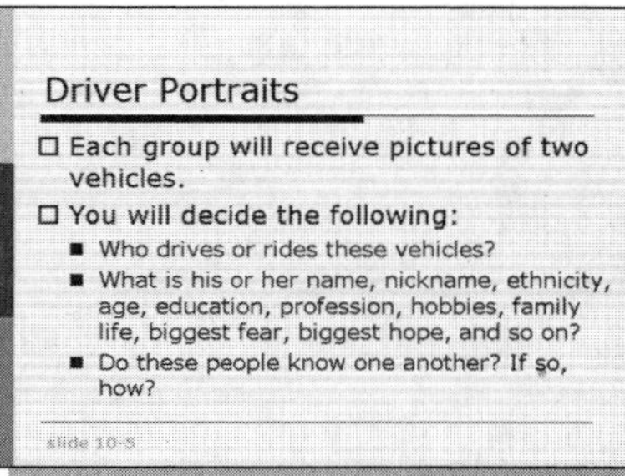

Driver Portraits
☐ Each group will receive pictures of two vehicles.
☐ You will decide the following:
■ Who drives or rides these vehicles?
■ What is his or her name, nickname, ethnicity, age, education, profession, hobbies, family life, biggest fear, biggest hope, and so on?
■ Do these people know one another? If so, how?
slide 10-5

Slide 10–6

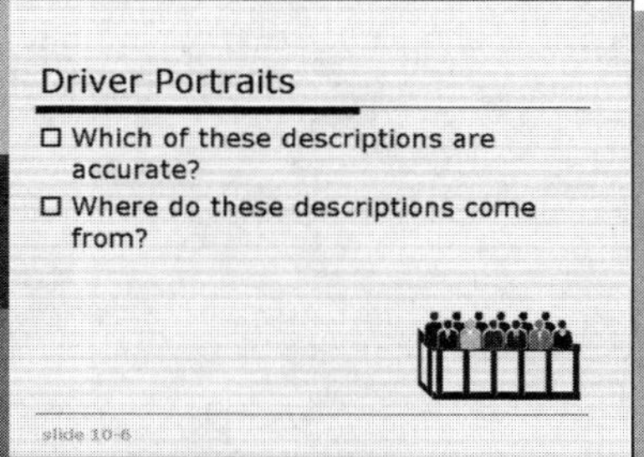

Driver Portraits
☐ Which of these descriptions are accurate?
☐ Where do these descriptions come from?
slide 10-6

Slide 10–7

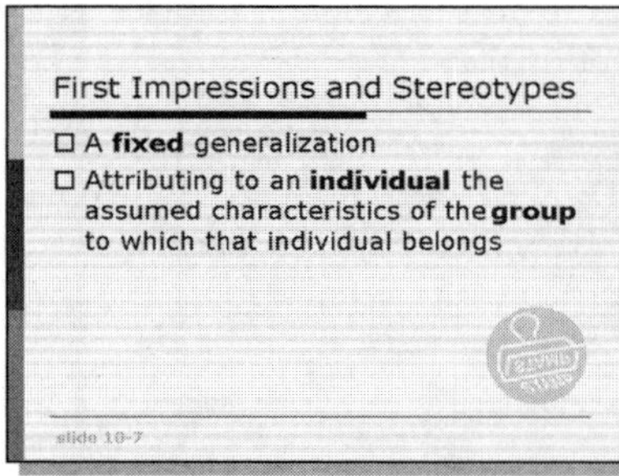

First Impressions and Stereotypes
☐ A fixed generalization
☐ Attributing to an individual the assumed characteristics of the group to which that individual belongs
slide 10-7

Slide 10–8

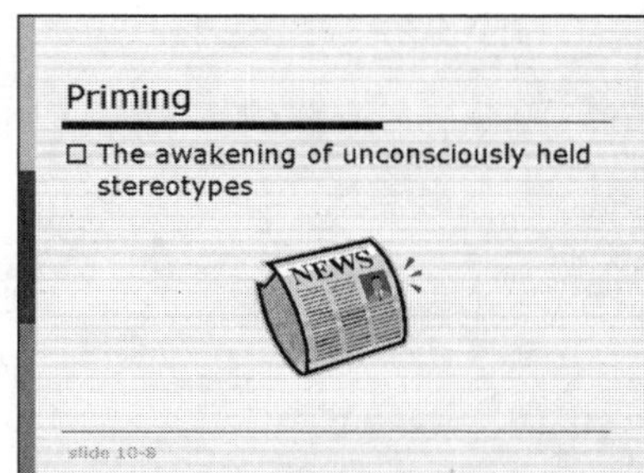

Priming
☐ The awakening of unconsciously held stereotypes
slide 10-8

Slide 10–9

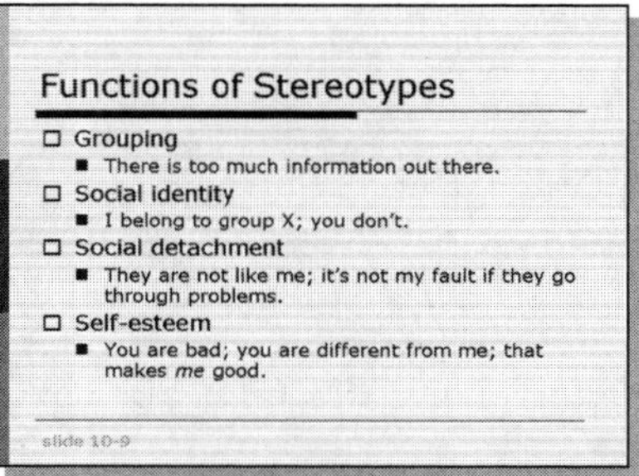

Functions of Stereotypes
☐ Grouping
■ There is too much information out there.
☐ Social identity
■ I belong to group X; you don't.
☐ Social detachment
■ They are not like me; it's not my fault if they go through problems.
☐ Self-esteem
■ You are bad; you are different from me; that makes me good.
slide 10-9

Slide 10–10

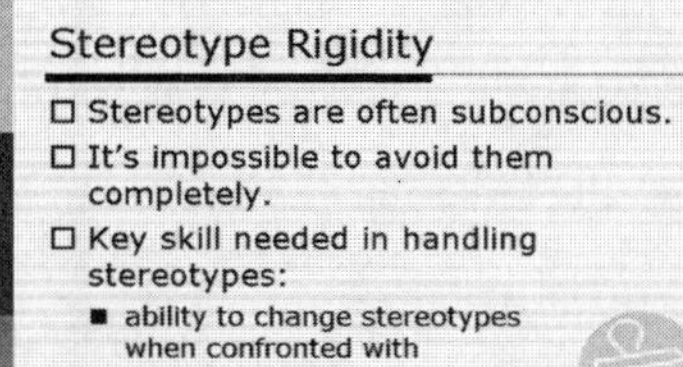

Stereotype Rigidity
☐ Stereotypes are often subconscious.
☐ It's impossible to avoid them completely.
☐ Key skill needed in handling stereotypes:
■ ability to change stereotypes when confronted with disproving evidence.
slide 10-10

Slide 10–11

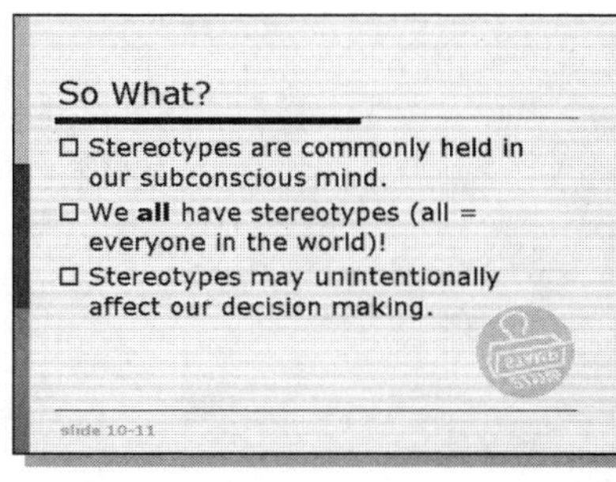

So What?
☐ Stereotypes are commonly held in our subconscious mind.
☐ We all have stereotypes (all = everyone in the world)!
☐ Stereotypes may unintentionally affect our decision making.
slide 10-11

Slide 10–12

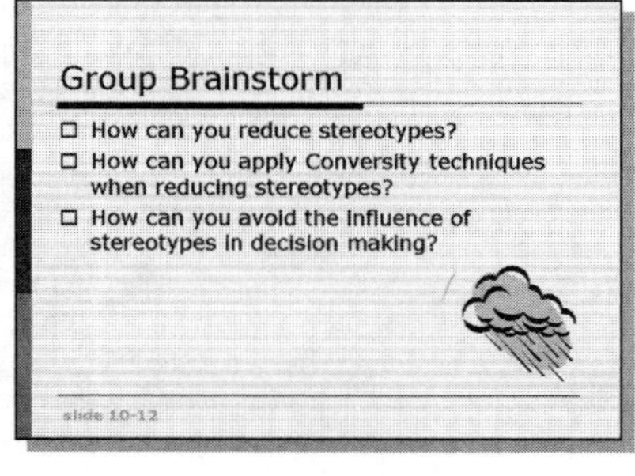

Group Brainstorm
☐ How can you reduce stereotypes?
☐ How can you apply Conversity techniques when reducing stereotypes?
☐ How can you avoid the influence of stereotypes in decision making?
slide 10-12

Slide 10–13

Disproving Stereotypes

- Who else could be driving those vehicles?
- How can you disprove stereotypes?
  - Bring up specific examples of people who disprove the stereotypes you came up with for the driver descriptions.

slide 10-13

Slide 10–14

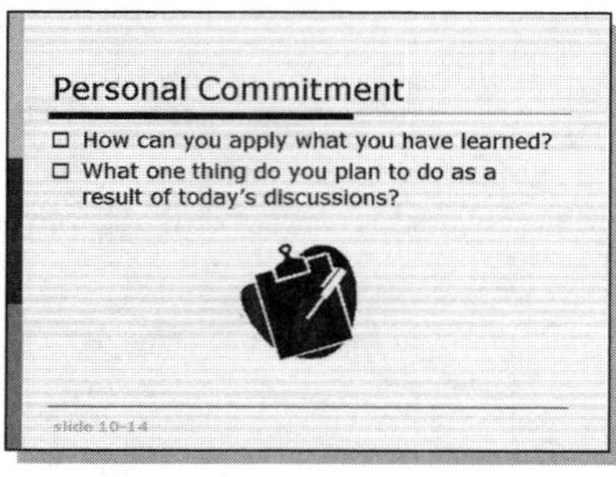

Personal Commitment
How can you apply what you have learned?
What one thing do you plan to do as a result of today's discussions?
slide 10-14

Chapter 11

Module 4: Walking in Their Shoes

What's in This Chapter?

- Objectives for the three-hour module on prejudice and discrimination
- Discussion of the legal safety of the instructional activities contained in the module
- List of materials for the facilitator and the participants
- Sample program agenda

Insanity in individuals is something rare—but in groups, parties, nations, and epochs, it is the rule.
– Friedrich Nietzsche (1844–1900), German philosopher

Module 4 introduces two key elements in diversity development: the origin of human prejudices and the relationship between prejudiced attitudes and subtle discriminatory behaviors.

This chapter gives you thorough instructions for running the module with small groups. Completing it should take you three to four hours. All instructions assume you will have a class of 20 participants, subdivided into four small groups of 5 members. If your group size is different, please adjust the quantities of materials accordingly.

When the training with this module has been completed, you may find it very useful to distribute to participants a diversity self-assessment. A simple one is available in this book—Assessment 13–1: Diversity Self-Awareness.

How Safe Is Module 4?

This module is the most sensitive of all modules presented in this workbook and it should be facilitated by experienced practitioners.

It is common for organizations to limit classroom discussions to visible *behaviors* and to avoid any discussions of prejudiced attitudes. Their argument is that it is inappropriate to address attitudes in the workplace.

The drawback to that approach is that attitudes and behaviors are interconnected. Moreover, modern discriminatory practices are often subtle, and it is very difficult to change them if the underlying attitudes are not addressed.

Of course, you may want to accept some risk in order to have a meaningful program. As in all other modules described in this book, you must use your own judgment and seek the advice of your legal counsel. If you choose to run this module, we suggest that you

- select a location away from the office
- run the program with a small group (no more than 20 people)
- divide sessions by organizational rank and separate managers from employees who report directly to them.

The last suggestion is given to protect the managers and the organization. For instance, in one exercise participants are asked to analyze what parents, peers, and other sources taught them about certain minority groups. This exercise was included because it is powerful and extremely useful to help participants decode their own prejudiced attitudes. On the other hand, it is not advisable for a manager to openly admit in front of others that he or she is prejudiced against a specific group.

This module will work better if an atmosphere of trust and comfort among participants and the facilitator(s) was established in the previous modules.

Training Objectives

The objectives for Module 4 are to help participants

- become aware of their own prejudices and connect them to life experiences and teachings
- explain the relationship between discrimination and prejudice

- describe and recognize subtle discriminatory behaviors involving body language, tone of voice, eye contact, and so forth.

Materials

There are several things you will need to facilitate this presentation. The list below will help you prepare properly.

For the instructor:

- Learning Activity 12–3: Personal Commitment
- Learning Activity 12–12: How Old Were You?
- Learning Activity 12–13: A New Product Line
- Learning Activity 12–14: The Company Picnic
- Learning Activity 12–15: Subtle Discrimination
- Tool 13–6: Group Banners, one set for each small group, cut into individual pieces and placed in an envelope
- Tool 13–7: Candidate Information Cards
- Projector, screen, and computer for running the PowerPoint presentation
- PowerPoint slides 11–1 through 11–22 (*Module 4.ppt* on the CD; thumbnail copies of the slides appear at the end of this chapter)
- A deck of playing cards

For the participants:

- Assessment 13–2: Sample Level 1 Evaluation
- Training Instrument 13–6: Personal Commitment Worksheet
- Training Instrument 13–7: Group Brainstorm
- Training Instrument 13–15: How Old Were You?
- Training Instrument 13–16: A New Product Line
- Training Instrument 13–17: A New Product Line—Discussion Sheet
- Training Instrument 13–18: The Company Picnic—Discussion Sheet
- Training Instrument 13–19: Subtle Discrimination—Discussion Sheet

Using the CD

Materials for this training session are provided in this workbook and as electronic files on the accompanying CD. To access the electronic files, insert the CD and click on the appropriate Adobe .pdf or PowerPoint .ppt/.pps files. Further directions and help using the files can be found in the appendix, "Using the Compact Disc," at the back of this workbook.

It's important that you review all of the slides as part of your preparation for the workshop. At that time you should plan explanations and examples for concepts presented in the slides.

As with all the other materials in this book, you may adapt the slides and handouts as long as you include in all your presentation materials the authors' names, company name, the title of this bookl, and copyright information.

Module 4 Sample Agenda

8:00 a.m. Welcome (5 minutes)

Display slide 11–1. Welcome participants and thank them for taking part in the session.

8:05 Review of Module 1 (10 minutes)

Display slide 11–2. Distribute a copy of Training Instrument 13–7 to each participant. Ask each group to use the questions on Training Instrument 13–7 as a guide for recapping the most important points presented in Module 3. Debrief discussions with the large group. Remind people that Conversity—finding common ground—should be a general theme for all diversity initiatives at the organization.

Note: Ideally, no new participants are coming onboard for this module. Maintaining the same roster of attendees increases the comfort level of the group and participants' ability to interact honestly with one another. If, however, you have new people, it is important to conduct a quick icebreaker and introductory activity. A fun one is to ask everyone to share the craziest thing they've ever done in their lives. It generates some laughs and starts your module on a good note.

8:15 Present the agenda (5 minutes)

Display slide 11–3. Explain that the main goal of this module is to discuss the connection between prejudice and discrimination. You may say, *Today we will explore our thoughts and feelings about groups different from our own. We will go through a variety of simulations and activities that will help us in that exploration. This is important because our thoughts and feelings are very much connected to the way we behave. It is impossible to address behaviors without understanding where they come from.*

Note: At this point you may want to explain that all humans are prejudiced against members of other groups. Refer participants to the lessons in Module 1: Out of the Box. Reassure them that the presence of prejudiced attitudes doesn't make anyone *bad* . . . simply human.

8:20 Learning Activity 12–12: How Old Were You? (20 minutes)

8:40 Learning Activity 12–13: A New Product Line (45 minutes)

9:25 Break (15 minutes)

9:40 Continue Learning Activity 12–13 (20 minutes)

Begin with step 5 in the instructions for Learning Activity 12–12.

10:00 Learning Activity 12–14: The Company Picnic (45 minutes)

10:45 Learning Activity 12–15: Subtle Discrimination (10 minutes)

10:55 Personal commitment (10 minutes)

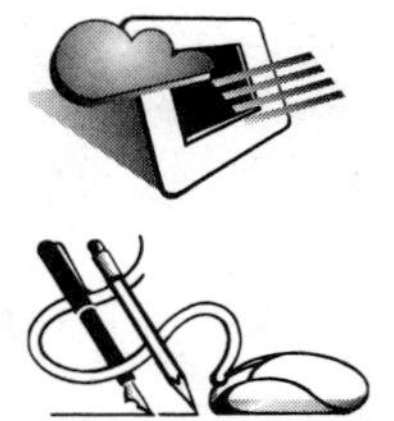

Display slide 11–22. Distribute a copy of Training Instrument 13–6: Personal Commitment Worksheet to each person. Ask participants to complete the worksheet individually.

If time is available, have members in small groups discuss their personal commitments and the main lessons learned in this session.

11:05 Conclusion and evaluation (5 minutes)

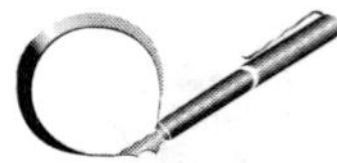

Make your concluding remarks. Thank participants for their efforts in the training session. Give a copy of Assessment 13–2: Sample Level 1 Evaluation to each person. Ask participants to complete the evaluation and place it on a table as they leave the room.

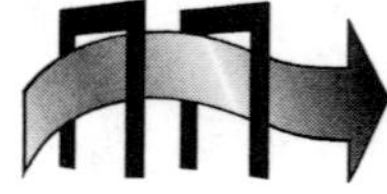

What to Do Next

- Gather materials to run this module with a small group of volunteers.
- Pilot-test the module and ask participants to give you feedback.
- Adjust the module according to the feedback you receive and the specific needs of your organization.
- Develop a process to encourage participants to share the commitments they have made with their supervisors or with a Conversity partner.

◆◆◆

This book was designed to give you a fully customizable set of modules and learning activities. Instead of running the modules as they were written, you may prefer to add some of the activities to your own program. The next chapter gives you a detailed explanation on how to run each of the activities described in Modules 1 through 4.

Slide 11–1

Conversity Leadership

Module 4: Walking in Their Shoes

Cris Wildermuth, M.Ed.
Susan D. Gray, PHR

Slide 11–2

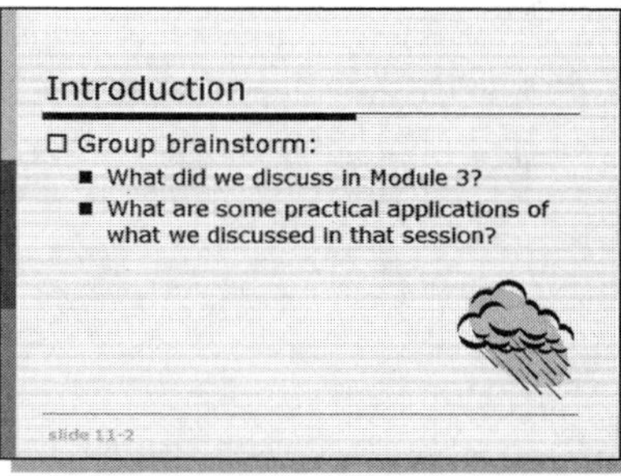

Introduction
□ Group brainstorm:
■ What did we discuss in Module 3?
■ What are some practical applications of what we discussed in that session?
slide 11-2

Slide 11–3

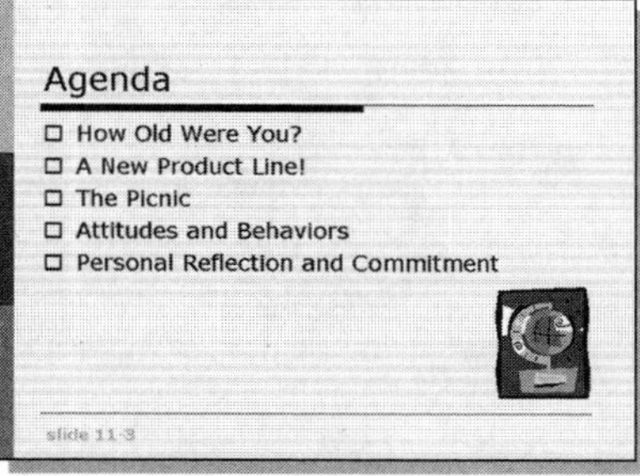

Agenda
□ How Old Were You?
□ A New Product Line!
□ The Picnic
□ Attitudes and Behaviors
□ Personal Reflection and Commitment
slide 11-3

Slide 11–4

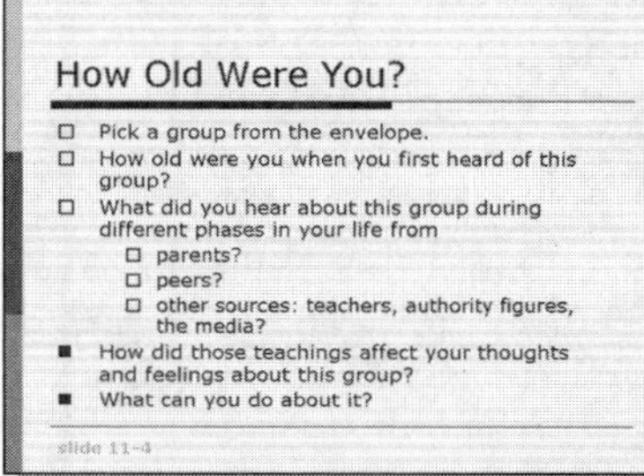

How Old Were You?
□ Pick a group from the envelope.
□ How old were you when you first heard of this group?
□ What did you hear about this group during different phases in your life from
□ parents?
□ peers?
□ other sources: teachers, authority figures, the media?
■ How did those teachings affect your thoughts and feelings about this group?
■ What can you do about it?
slide 11-4

Slide 11–5

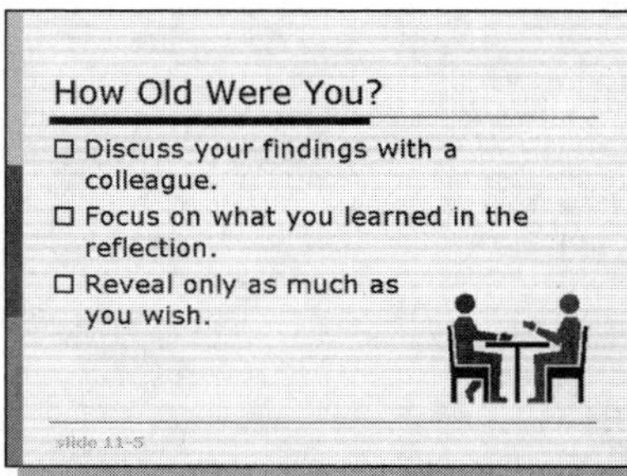

How Old Were You?
□ Discuss your findings with a colleague.
□ Focus on what you learned in the reflection.
□ Reveal only as much as you wish.
slide 11-5

Slide 11–6

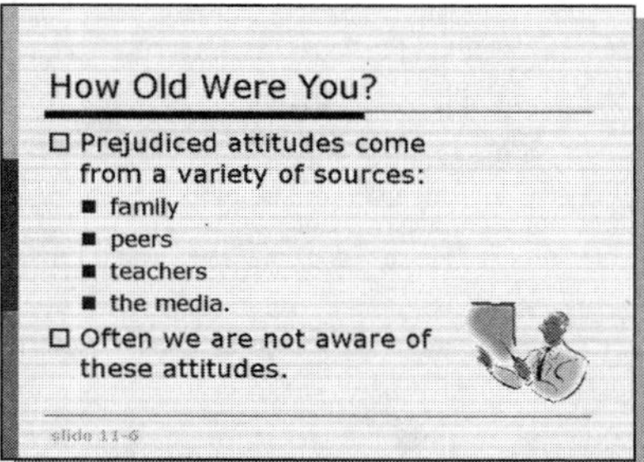

How Old Were You?
□ Prejudiced attitudes come from a variety of sources:
■ family
■ peers
■ teachers
■ the media.
□ Often we are not aware of these attitudes.
slide 11-6

Slide 11–7

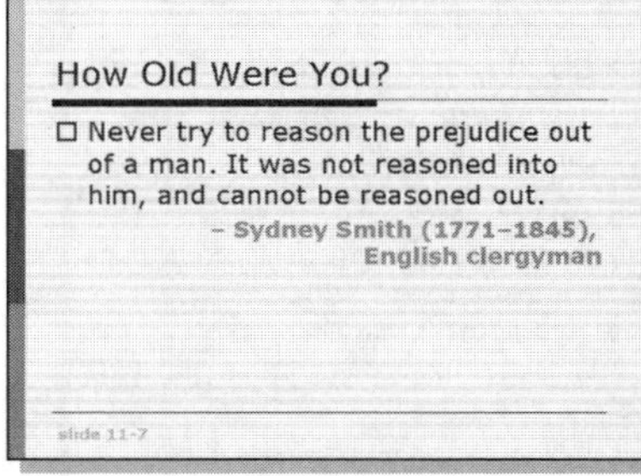

How Old Were You?
□ Never try to reason the prejudice out of a man. It was not reasoned into him, and cannot be reasoned out.
– Sydney Smith (1771–1845), English clergyman
slide 11-7

Slide 11–8

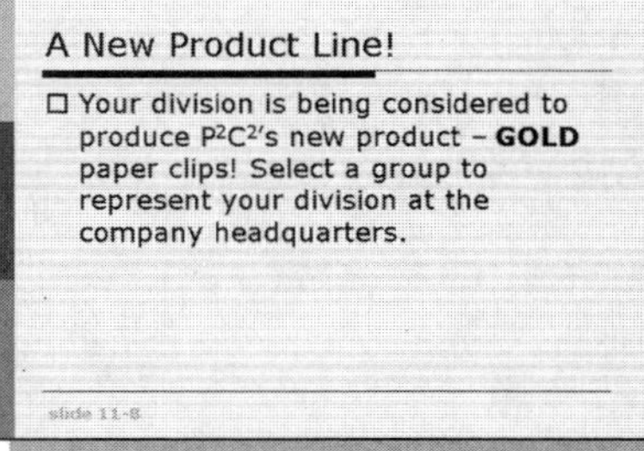

A New Product Line!
□ Your division is being considered to produce P²C²'s new product – GOLD paper clips! Select a group to represent your division at the company headquarters.
slide 11-8

Slide 11–9

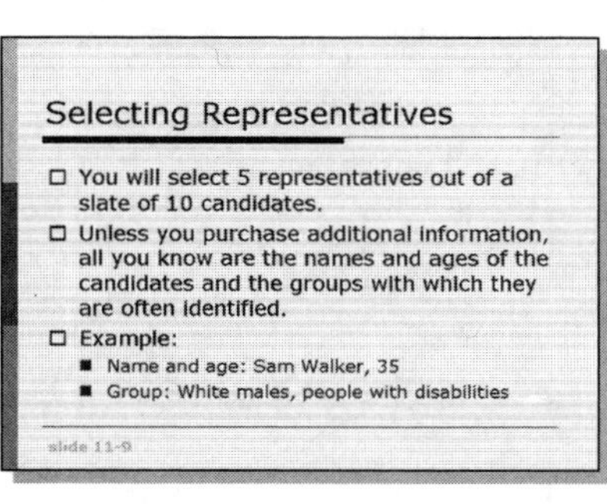

Selecting Representatives
□ You will select 5 representatives out of a slate of 10 candidates.
□ Unless you purchase additional information, all you know are the names and ages of the candidates and the groups with which they are often identified.
□ Example:
■ Name and age: Sam Walker, 35
■ Group: White males, people with disabilities
slide 11-9

Slide 11–10

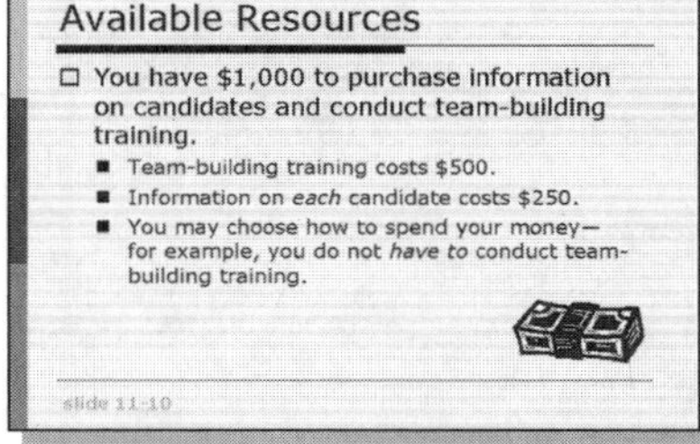

Available Resources
□ You have $1,000 to purchase information on candidates and conduct team-building training.
■ Team-building training costs $500.
■ Information on each candidate costs $250.
■ You may choose how to spend your money—for example, you do not have to conduct team-building training.
slide 11-10

Slide 11–11

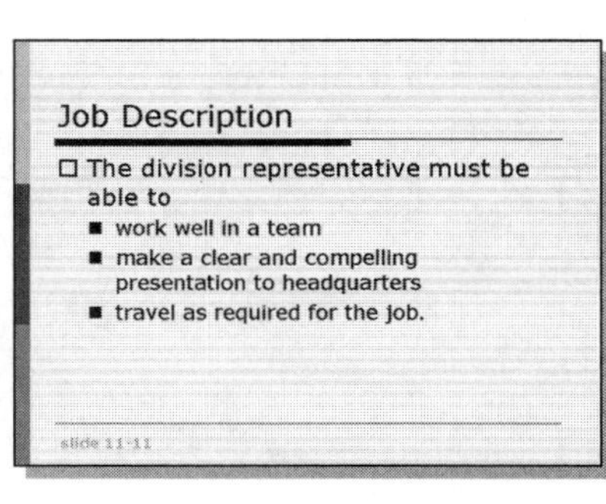

Job Description
□ The division representative must be able to
■ work well in a team
■ make a clear and compelling presentation to headquarters
■ travel as required for the job.
slide 11-11

Slide 11–12

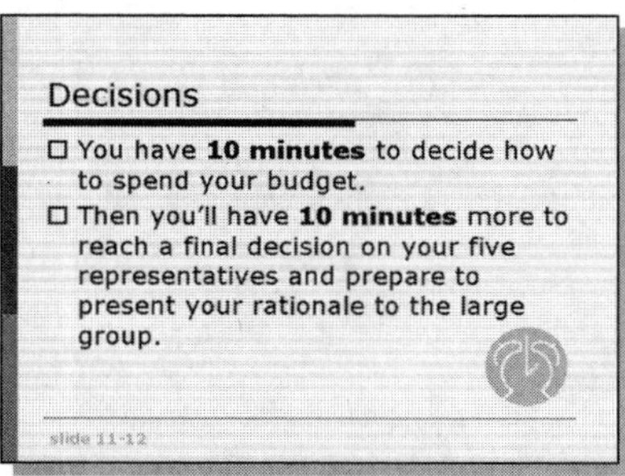

Decisions
□ You have 10 minutes to decide how to spend your budget.
□ Then you'll have 10 minutes more to reach a final decision on your five representatives and prepare to present your rationale to the large group.
slide 11-12

Slide 11–13

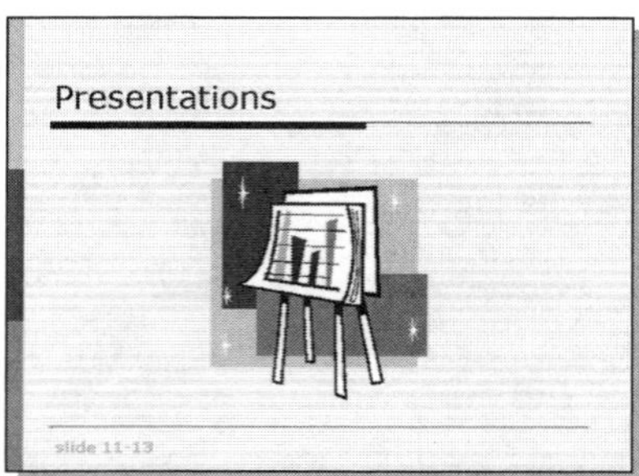

Slide 11–14

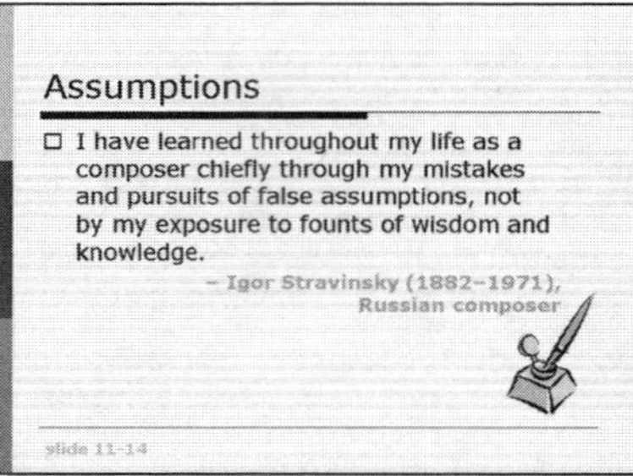

Assumptions
I have learned throughout my life as a composer chiefly through my mistakes and pursuits of false assumptions, not by my exposure to founts of wisdom and knowledge.
– Igor Stravinsky (1882–1971), Russian composer
slide 11-14

Slide 11–15

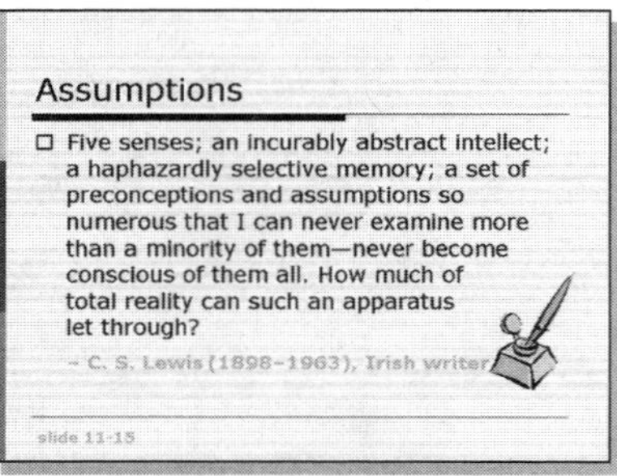

Assumptions
Five senses; an incurably abstract intellect; a haphazardly selective memory; a set of preconceptions and assumptions so numerous that I can never examine more than a minority of them—never become conscious of them all. How much of total reality can such an apparatus let through?
– C. S. Lewis (1898–1963), Irish writer
slide 11-15

Slide 11–16

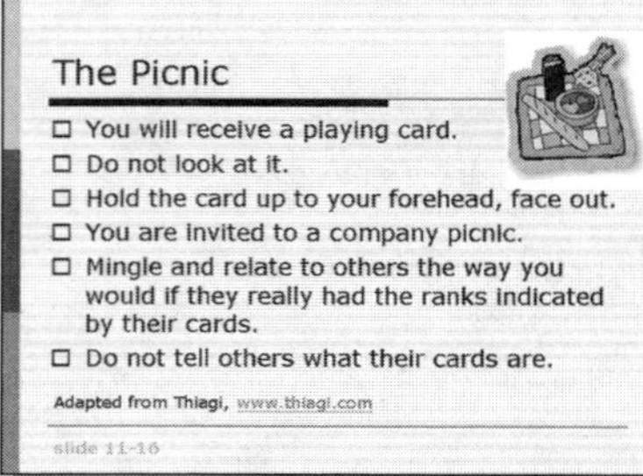

The Picnic
You will receive a playing card.
Do not look at it.
Hold the card up to your forehead, face out.
You are invited to a company picnic.
Mingle and relate to others the way you would if they really had the ranks indicated by their cards.
Do not tell others what their cards are.
Adapted from Thiagi, www.thiagi.com
slide 11-16

Slide 11–17

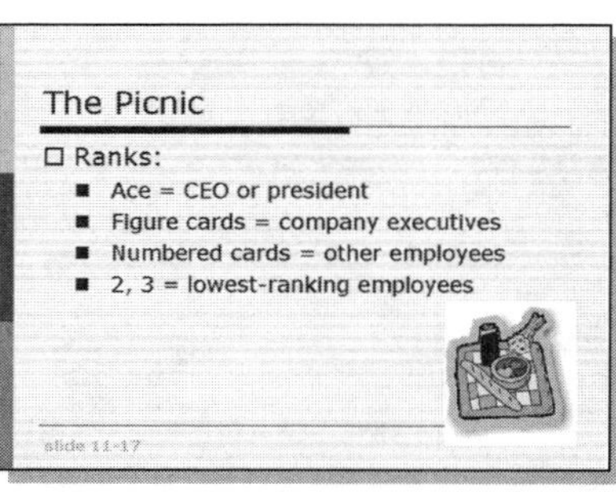

The Picnic
Ranks:
Ace = CEO or president
Figure cards = company executives
Numbered cards = other employees
2, 3 = lowest-ranking employees
slide 11-17

Slide 11–18

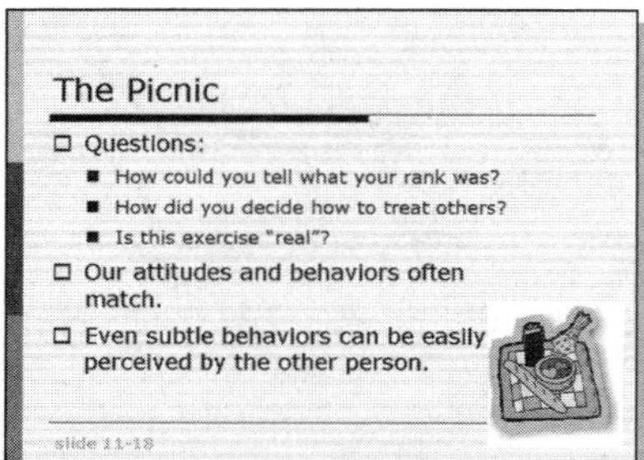

The Picnic
Questions:
How could you tell what your rank was?
How did you decide how to treat others?
Is this exercise "real"?
Our attitudes and behaviors often match.
Even subtle behaviors can be easily perceived by the other person.
slide 11-18

Slide 11–19

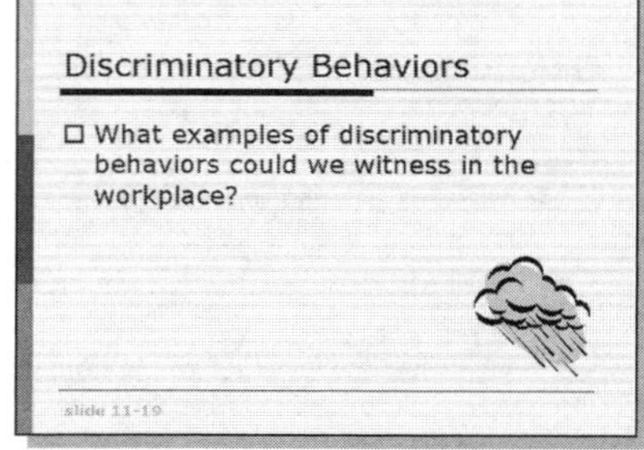

Discriminatory Behaviors
What examples of discriminatory behaviors could we witness in the workplace?
slide 11-19

Slide 11–20

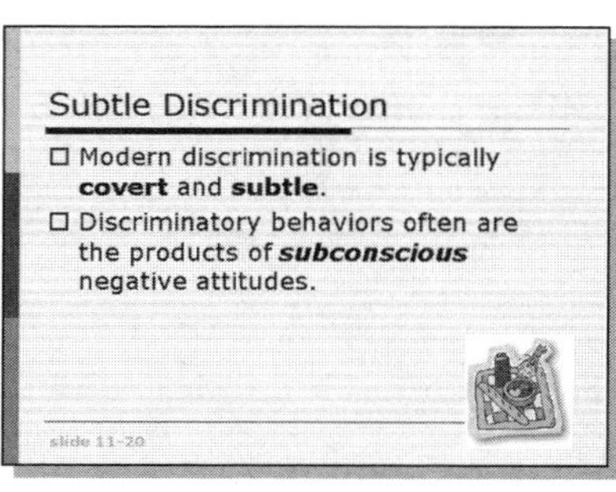

Subtle Discrimination
Modern discrimination is typically covert and subtle.
Discriminatory behaviors often are the products of subconscious negative attitudes.
slide 11-20

Slide 11–21

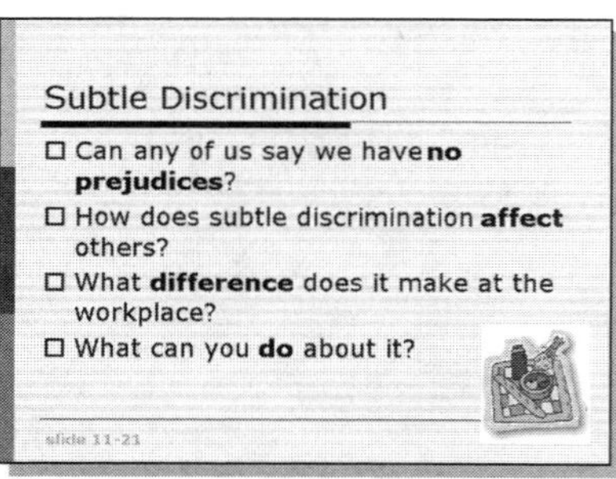

Subtle Discrimination
Can any of us say we have no prejudices?
How does subtle discrimination affect others?
What difference does it make at the workplace?
What can you do about it?
slide 11-21

Slide 11–22

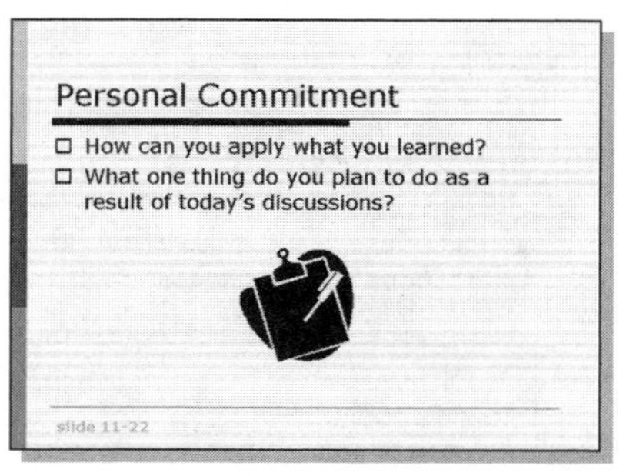

Personal Commitment
How can you apply what you learned?
What one thing do you plan to do as a result of today's discussions?
slide 11-22

Chapter 12

Learning Activities

What's in This Chapter?

- Fifteen learning activities for use in the training sessions
- Definitive goals for all activities
- Complete step-by-step instructions for conducting the learning activities

This chapter, which includes all the learning activities used in Modules 1 through 4, will be particularly useful if you prefer to create your own program agendas from what is offered in this book, instead of following the complete modular sequences provided in chapters 8 through 11. If you choose to customize any of these activities to adapt them to your own needs, please include the proper attributions (the authors' names, the title of this workbook, and the copyright information).

Adjust and adapt these activities to fit your own needs and objectives. We strongly recommend that you pilot-test all simulations prior to your program. Test them, adjust the timing and content to your own style, and rewrite them in whatever way makes sense to you.

Here's a list of the activities we'll cover in detail in this chapter:

- Learning Activity 12–1: The P^2C^2 Challenge, Parts I and II
- Learning Activity 12–2: Seeking Connections
- Learning Activity 12–3: Personal Commitment
- Learning Activity 12–4: The Interview
- Learning Activity 12–5: Your Cultural Continuum

- Learning Activity 12–6: Values Line
- Learning Activity 12–7: Value Congruency
- Learning Activity 12–8: Value Decision Making
- Learning Activity 12–9: Figuring Things Out
- Learning Activity 12–10: Driver Portraits
- Learning Activity 12–11: Disproving Stereotypes
- Learning Activity 12–12: How Old Were You?
- Learning Activity 12–13: A New Product Line
- Learning Activity 12–14: The Company Picnic
- Learning Activity 12–15: Subtle Discrimination

Learning Activity 12–1: The P^2C^2 Challenge, Parts I and II

GOAL

The goal of this simulation is to help participants experience the strength of the bonds that connect groups—bonds that often cause human beings to discriminate against members of other groups and to try to allocate more resources to members of their own group. Participants will

- experience social identity bias or the tendency to prioritize the interests of one's own group
- examine personal biases toward members of other groups.

MATERIALS

- 20 paper clips or other small objects in four different colors
- Two additional jars of 20 paper clips each (total of 40 paper clips or two times the number of participants)
- Training Instrument 13–3: Welcome to P^2C^2 (one per participant)
- Training Instrument 13–4: Windfall! (one per participant)
- Training Instrument 13–5: The P^2C^2 Challenge (one per participant)
- PowerPoint slides 8–4 through 8–9 **(To access** the slides for this learning activity, open the PowerPoint file *Module 1.ppt/pps* on the accompanying CD. Thumbnail copies of the slides are included at the end of chapter 8.)

TIME

- 90 minutes

INSTRUCTIONS

Part I: Welcome to P^2C^2

1. Describe the scenario (5 minutes)

- Distribute to each participant a copy of Training Instrument 13–3: Welcome to P^2C^2 and display slide 8–4. Read the scenario and the instructions aloud or have participants read on their own.

- You may want to emphasize that participants no longer work for their own organization—they are all now employees of P^2C^2, where paper clips are both the products and the currency. They are used as bonuses, incentives, and salary increases.
- **Tip:** To illustrate the idea that paper clips are the new currency, put on a paper clip necklace or tie tac and decorate the room with paper clip strings or pictures. Whatever you do to get participants to *want* paper clips is beneficial. For example, you might have small prizes available to award at the end of the session to participants who manage to accumulate the most paper clips.

2. Explain the mission and have participants form groups (5 minutes)

- Display slide 8–5.
- Explain that participants need to prepare a *persuasive* presentation. Tell them that the job of each group is to convince a distinguished panel of judges that it is the most deserving group to win a jar of paper clips. Tell participants each group will have 10 minutes to prepare its presentation.

- Display slide 8–6.
- Pass around a jar with as many paper clips (or other small objects you choose to use in this activity) as you have participants, equally divided by color into as many participant groups as you plan to have. Ask participants to quickly pick up a paper clip and form groups. *Don't* tell them *how* to form their groups. They are most likely to look for others holding a piece of a similar color. That decision may be an interesting source of discussion later on.

3. Have groups work on their presentations (10 minutes)

- Give groups 10 minutes to develop their convincing presentations that are three to four minutes in length. Also instruct them to choose a representative to serve on the panel of judges and another person to speak to the panel on their group's behalf.

4. Have each group's spokesperson plead its case and then ask the panel to vote (20 minutes)

- Display slide 8–7.
- Form the panel of judges with representatives from each group.

- Have group spokespeople present their cases.
- Ask judges to deliberate and present a decision.
- Award the jar of paper clips to the chosen group.
- **An option:** At this point you might interrupt the simulation and debrief it by asking questions, such as

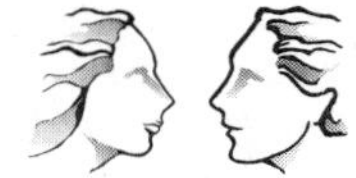

  1. How did it feel to win or lose the jar of clips?
  2. How fair were the judges?
  3. How fair was the ultimate distribution of clips?
  4. How do you feel toward members of your own group now?
  5. How likely were you to collaborate with another group's efforts during the exercise?
  6. What does this exercise have to do with real life?

Part II: Windfall!

1. Describe the scenario (5 minutes)

   - Display slide 8–8.
   - Distribute a copy of Training Instrument 13–4: Windfall! to each participant.
   - Explain that the board of directors has 20 additional paper clips to distribute and each group must design a distribution system and present it to the whole class.
   - Have groups reconvene to decide how to distribute this windfall of additional clips.
   - Tell participants they have five minutes to deliberate and that each group's spokesperson must make his or her presentation in only one minute.

2. Have participants devise distribution plans (5 minutes)
   - Tell groups to discuss appropriate solutions.
   - Avoid giving too many instructions at this point because the decision of each group can be discussed later during the debriefing.

3. Ask the spokesperson from each group to present its plan (5 minutes)

   - Ask them to explain their group's suggested solution and the rationale behind it. Limit each presentation to no more than one minute.

4. Ask the panel of judges to select the winning distribution plan (5 minutes).

   - Ask the judges empowered in Part I to decide who wins the extra paper clips. Award the winning group the paper clips.
   - **Time-saving alternative:** Skip the judges' deliberations and go straight to the group discussion that follows. What is important at this point is not who won but how decisions were made and how groups felt while making them.

5. Enable group discussion (10 minutes)

   - Display slide 8–9.
   - Give a copy of Training Instrument 13–5: The P^2C^2 Challenge to each person. Ask participants to elect a facilitator in each group. This person will guide discussion, take notes, and report on findings during debriefing.

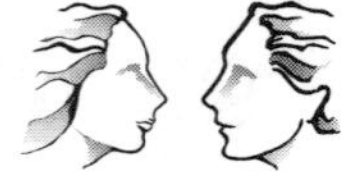

   - Explain that each group will have eight minutes to answer the questions on the slide. Tell facilitators that their debriefing presentations can be no more than one minute.
   - **Time-saving alternative:** Instead of having each team present a report of its findings, go straight to a general discussion of the exercise.

6. Hold a general debriefing session (15 minutes)

   - Ask each group facilitator to present a one-minute summary of the group's findings.
   - Facilitate a general discussion about the overall experience.
   - Probe deeper into participants' feelings about members of other groups. Possible additional discussion questions include

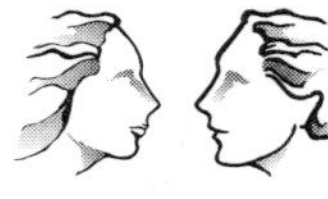

     a. Would you allow a member of another group to participate in your discussions?

b. If you had the opportunity to hire someone, would you rather hire a member of your group or a member of another group? Why?

◆ **Tips:**

1. Allow enough time in the P^2C^2 simulation and its debriefing for participants to strengthen their bonds to their own groups.

2. Anything you can do to encourage competition during the simulation will be beneficial.

3. Remind people how they formed groups in the first place. Very often participants seek others whose paper clip colors are the same as theirs. Ask them about their rationale for group division and why they didn't seek others with different paper clip colors.

4. After the simulation, display slide 8–11 and discuss the impact of informal social networks in the workplace. Emphasize that it is important for people to be aware of how their in-group biases influence their behavior at work. Often we are not aware that we treat people differently, depending on whether they are perceived as belonging to our group.

Learning Activity 12–2: Seeking Connections

GOAL

The goal of this activity is to help participants experience Conversity, or the ability to intentionally find connections with others.

MATERIALS

- Training Instrument 13–1: Introducing Conversity
- PowerPoint slides 8–12 through 8–16 (To access the slides for this learning activity, open the PowerPoint file *Module 1.ppt/pps* on the accompanying CD. Thumbnail copies of the slides are included at the end of chapter 8.)

TIME

- 25 minutes

INSTRUCTIONS

1. Facilitate a general discussion (5 minutes)

   - Display slide 8–12.
   - Remind participants that having a positive bias toward one's own group is a normal human reaction. Note, however, that bias influences people's chances for success at work. Ask participants for possible solutions to this dilemma.

2. Introduce Conversity (5 minutes)

   - Display slides 8–13 and 8–14. Explain that one key to overcoming in-group bias is to form new, all-encompassing groups. Through Conversity it is possible to perceive more connections than differences. When people find connections, they are able to perceive themselves as belonging to the same group.

3. Facilitate Conversity dialogues and debrief the experience (15 minutes)

   - Display slide 8–5. and distribute a copy of Training Instrument 13–1: Introducing Conversity to each participant.

- Have participants pair up and look for similarities between them. Encourage them to go beyond the obvious and search for hidden similarities.

- Display slide 8–16.
- Debrief the activity by asking participants to share some of the similarities they found. Ask how this activity might be reproduced in the workplace.

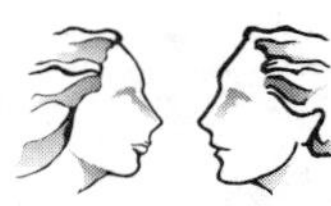

- **Tip:** Use the last question in Training Instrument 13–1 to discuss the possible payoff of Conversity dialogues in the workplace. Explain that these dialogues may be informal. The idea is to try continuously to find connections with colleagues, even if those connections are not obvious or work-related.

Learning Activity 12–3: Personal Commitment

GOAL

The goal of this activity is to help participants apply in their work environment what they learn in the module.

MATERIALS

- Training Instrument 13–6: Personal Commitment Worksheet
- PowerPoint slide 8–17 (To access the slide for this learning activity, open the PowerPoint file *Module 1.ppt/pps* on the accompanying CD. A thumbnail copy of the slide is included at the end of chapter 8.)

TIME

- 10 minutes

INSTRUCTIONS

- Display slide 8–17.
- Distribute a copy of Training Instrument 13–6 to each participant.
- Ask participants to complete their Personal Commitment Worksheets individually.
- If time is available, ask the members of the small groups to discuss their personal commitments and what they learned in the session.

Learning Activity 12–4: The Interview

GOAL

The goal of this activity is to help participants experience the impact of cultural rules on behaviors at work and on their own decision making.

MATERIALS

- Training Instrument 13–8: The Interview
- Tool 13–1: Interviewer Questions
- Tool 13–2: Cultural Rules Card Set (cut sheets apart to create individual cards)
- PowerPoint slides 9–4 through 9–6 (To access the slides for this learning activity, open the PowerPoint file *Module 2.ppt/pps* on the accompanying CD. Thumbnail copies of the slides are included at the end of chapter 9.)

TIME

- 40 minutes

INSTRUCTIONS

1. Set up the scenario (10 minutes)

   - Distribute Training Instrument 13–8: The Interview, and describe the scenario to the group.

   - Display slide 9–4. Ask for four volunteers: one to be the interviewer and three to be job candidates.

   - Give the interviewer a copy of Tool 13–1, which he or she will use to ask the questions of the candidates.

   - Give each candidate one card from Tool 13–2: Cultural Rules Card Set. Instruct the candidates not to share the information on their cards with anyone else. Explain to them that they will use the rules on the card as the basis for all of their answers to the interviewer's questions.

- Suggest to the remaining participants that they take notes as they listen to the candidates' answers during the interviews because they will be serving as the hiring committee.
- Ask volunteers to come to the front of the room and take their seats for the interviews.
- **Tip:** Role plays are intimidating for some participants and highly enjoyable for others. If you don't know the participants well, ask if anyone in the room has some drama experience (even high school or college productions count.) If you prefer, run this exercise in a couple of smaller groups.

2. Conduct the interview (10 minutes)

- Have the interviewer ask the same questions of each candidate.

3. Hiring committee discussion (10 minutes)

- Display slide 9–5 and direct participants who form the hiring committee to the questions at the end of Training Instrument 13–8.
- Ask them to discuss their observations and decide which candidate they would hire.

4. Debrief the experience (10 minutes)

- Ask members of the hiring committee to report on their decision and how they arrived at it.
- Have candidates share with the whole class the cultural rules under which they operated in answering the questions.
- Help participants understand that people are more likely to select the interviewee whose cultural rules match their own.

- Display slide 9–6 and explain that culture is a set of instructions—often unwritten—that is learned over a period of many years.

Learning Activity 12–5: Your Cultural Continuum

GOAL

The goal of this activity is to help participants examine their own cultural preferences and contrast them to the preferences of the average member of their culture.

MATERIALS

- Training Instrument 13–9: Your Cultural Continuum
- PowerPoint slides 9–10 through 9–12 (To access the slides for this learning activity, open the PowerPoint file *Module 2.ppt/pps* on the accompanying CD. Thumbnail copies of the slides are included at the end of chapter 9.)

TIME

- 35 minutes

INSTRUCTIONS

1. Explain the activity (5 minutes)

   - Display slide 9–10 and distribute a copy of Training Instrument 13–9 to each participant.

   - Read with participants the instructions in the first paragraph.

   - Display slide 9–11. Reinforce the instructions using the animation in the slide.
2. Elicit individual responses (5 minutes). Have participants complete the instrument individually.
3. Discuss in small groups (10 minutes). Ask participants to discuss their individual responses with their small groups. Recommend that they explain how they individually differ from the norms of their culture.
4. Debrief the experience (15 minutes)

   - Display slide 9–12 and ask the questions that appear there.

- Facilitate a discussion of the impact of cultural dimensions on the work setting.

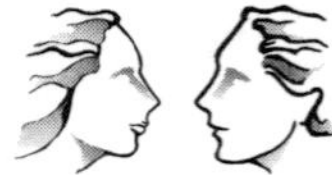

- **Tip:** You may want to ask specific questions on how each dimension influences relationships at work. For instance, what happens if someone who prefers an indirect style of communication works with someone whose style is very direct? What is the effect of having someone in the group who strongly dislikes conflict? How does a lack of punctuality affect someone's career in the United States? How could these cultural dimensions influence someone's chances of being promoted?

Learning Activity 12-6: Values Line

GOAL

The goal of this activity is to help participants visualize and experience value differences among members of the same culture.

MATERIALS

- PowerPoint slides 9–13 and 9–14 (To access the slides for this learning activity, open the PowerPoint file *Module 2.ppt/pps* on the accompanying CD. Thumbnail copies of the slides are included at the end of chapter 9.)

TIME

- 10 minutes

INSTRUCTIONS

1. Explain the activity (5 minutes)

   - Display slide 9–13.
   - Have participants stand as a group and come to the middle of the room.
   - Explain that you will give them pairs of words and that each person will move around the room, depending on which of the two words he or she considers more important. Instruct them to move to the right if they choose the first word, move to the left if they choose the second word, or remain in the middle if they judge the two words to be of equal importance to them.

     Here are some pairs of words that work well for this exercise:

     - harmony/conflict
     - privacy/hospitality
     - family/money
     - religion/family.

     After each pair of words and each accompanying movement, point out how participants have prioritized words differently by asking everyone to notice how people are positioned. For example, in a group of 20, you may have nine people who moved toward privacy, four who moved toward hospitality, and eight who remained in the middle. Each pair of words is likely to produce a new pattern.

2. Brief lecture on values (5 minutes)

- Display slide 9–14.
- Explain that our values are beliefs about what is *most* important to us. Add that a value often can only be defined by comparison. For instance, most participants would probably agree that all concepts brought up during the Values Line exercise—harmony, privacy, hospitality, family, religion, and money—are important. But which are *most* important? Even though everyone may agree, for instance, that both religion and family are important, some people may believe that religion is more important than family and others that family is more important than religion.
- **Note:** You may want to remind participants of the Conversity ideas taught in Module 1. Ask them how Conversity might be used in a values discussion, considering that values are what is *most* important to an individual. *Here's a possible answer:* There is common ground to be found in most values discussions, primarily in the matter of degree. For instance, even people for whom punctuality is not the *most* important value will probably agree that punctuality has *some* merit. People who believe that punctuality is *more* important than building relationships with others will likely agree that relationships are at least somewhat important. Acknowledging the significance of one another's values may initiate a positive dialogue.

Learning Activity 12–7: Value Congruency

GOALS

The goals of this activity are to help participants become aware of their own values, assess the level of contrast (that is, value congruency) between their values and those of their organization, and discuss the personal and team impact of such contrast.

MATERIALS

- Tool 12–1: Value Congruency Sample
- Training Instrument 13–10: Value Congruency
- PowerPoint slides 9–15 through 9–18 (To access the slides for this learning activity, open the PowerPoint file *Module 2.ppt/pps* on the accompanying CD. Thumbnail copies of the slides are included at the end of chapter 9.)

TIME

- 45 minutes

INSTRUCTIONS

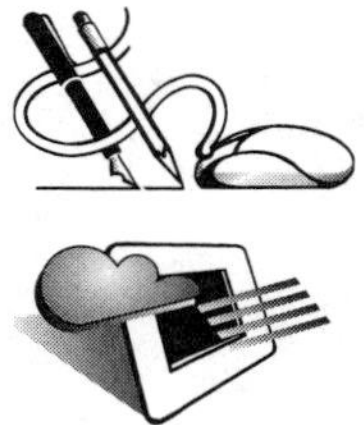

1. Explain the activity (5 minutes)
    - Distribute a copy of Training Instrument 13–10 to each person.
    - Display slides 9–15 through 9–17.
    - Describe the scenario and explain the parts of the activity by enumerating the instructions on the slides or the handout.
    - **Note:** Customize this activity to match your organization's needs by changing the items in the Values column of the training instrument or by changing the amount of money that participants have to distribute.
2. Participants fund their values individually (5 minutes)
    - Ask participants to divide $20 among the values appearing on the left side of the chart. They should write in Column A those

amounts they personally would give to each value (including zero, if applicable).

- Remind them that the money doesn't need to be divided equally.

- **Tip:** Tool 12–1 (page 134) is a sample Value Congruency table. You may want to enlarge it to poster size or copy it onto a flipchart as an example for the class. Before displaying it, write your own funding decisions in Column A.

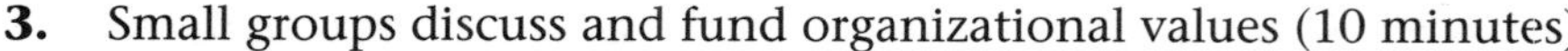

3. Small groups discuss and fund organizational values (10 minutes)

- Ask participants to reach a consensus on how *the organization* would assign the same $20 to those values.
- Remind them that they must agree on the distribution.
- Suggest that they *not vote* to reach a decision, but instead discuss until they can agree on amounts of money for each value.
- When final decisions have been reached, ask someone to read each group's amounts aloud. Direct each participant to write those amounts in Column B on their own handouts. At the same time, write the amounts on your flipchart example.

4. Calculate individual value congruencies (5 minutes)

- Ask participants to subtract the lesser amount given to each value from the greater amount given. Model this subtraction on your flipchart example.
- Explain that plus or minus signs are not needed. The significant result is the degree of difference between personal and organizational values, not whether that difference is positive or negative.
- Ask participants to add up the values in Column C. Explain that the value congruency level is the difference between their value assignments and those of the organization as a whole. The smaller the number in the Total box in Column C, the more aligned their own value system is with that of the organization.

5. Facilitate group discussions (10 minutes)

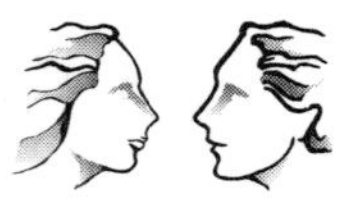

- Ask groups to discuss the questions at the end of the training instrument and get ready to report their findings.

6. Participants share their findings (10 minutes)

   - Display slide 9–18.
   - Facilitate a general discussion of the questions the small groups have just addressed.
   - **Creative option:** Even though actual money is not necessary for this activity, you may want to distribute play money as a reminder of the lessons learned in the exercise.

Tool 12–1
Value Congruency Sample

	A	B	C
VALUE	HOW YOU RANK THIS VALUE	HOW THE ORGANIZATION RANKS THIS VALUE	VALUE CONGRUENCY
Balance between work and family	3	3	0
Recognition	2	3	1
Innovation	4	0	4
Profits/compensation	4	5	1
Continuous learning	5	1	4
Community involvement	0	1	1
Stability	0	0	0
Integrity	2	4	2
Diversity	0	0	0
Equality	0	3	3
Total			**16**

Learning Activity 12–8: Value Decision Making

GOAL

The goal of this activity is to help participants experience the impact of value differences on decision making in the workplace.

MATERIALS

- Tool 13–3: Values Card Set (cut sheets apart to produce separate cards)
- Training Instrument 13–11: Value Decision Making
- PowerPoint slides 9–19 and 9–20 (To access the slides for this learning activity, open the PowerPoint file *Module 2.ppt/pps* on the accompanying CD. Thumbnail copies of the slides are included at the end of chapter 9.)

TIME

- 25 minutes

INSTRUCTIONS

1. Explain the activity (5 minutes)

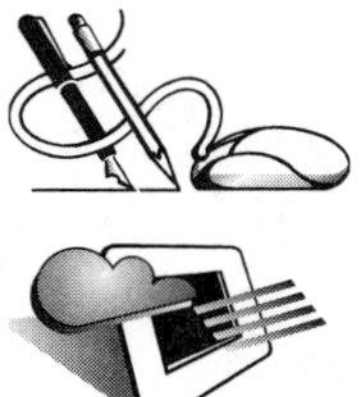

- Distribute Training Instrument 13–11: Value Decision Making and display slide 9–19.
- Use the slide or the instructions on the handout to explain the exercise. You may say, *Sometimes we get confused and bewildered by someone's inability to see things our way. It is important to remember that most people's decisions are logical, even if we can't understand their logic.*
- Read the scenario presented in the handout. Explain that each participant will operate according to one key value expressed on the values card he or she draws from the stack. Ask participants not to share the content of their cards. Place one set of value cards (Tool 13–3) face down on each table, and ask participants to pick one card from the pile.

2. Hold small-group discussions (10 minutes)

   - Appoint a leader and an observer in each group. (**Tip:** A fun way to do that is to say, *The leader and the observer are the last two people who stand!* Then just wait. Eventually people catch on and scramble to get up as quickly as possible.) Explain that the leader must coordinate the group discussion and the observer should take notes on how the group interacts. Tell participants they have 10 minutes to answer the three questions on the training instrument.

3. Debrief the experience (10 minutes)

   - Display slide 9–20.
   - Use questions on the slide to facilitate a general debriefing of the activity.
   - **Note:** If you have a large group, you may choose to have small groups discuss the questions on slide 9–20 before the general debriefing. If you choose this option, you will need to adjust the time accordingly. Each small group should have about 10 minutes to discuss the experience before a general debriefing. The debriefing then would require an additional 10 minutes.

Learning Activity 12–9: Figuring Things Out

GOAL

The goal of this activity is to give participants practice in using nonjudgmental language when discussing issues that may be influenced by people's cultures and value systems.

MATERIALS

- Training Instrument 13–12: Figuring Things Out
- PowerPoint slides 9–21 through 9–25 (To access the slides for this learning activity, open the PowerPoint file *Module 2.ppt/pps* on the accompanying CD. Thumbnail copies of the slides are included at the end of chapter 9.)

TIME

- 25 minutes

INSTRUCTIONS

1. Set the scene and explain the exercise (5 minutes)

- Distribute a copy of Training Instrument 13–12: Figuring Things Out to each participant.
- Read or paraphrase the information in the first paragraph.

- Display slide 9–21 and read the scenario.
- Display slide 9–22.
- Share with participants interpretation #1 and ask the corresponding question. Point out that the assumption that John is a slacker is obvious in the wording of the question. The person asking the question assumes he or she already knows the answer.

- Display slide 9–23 and share interpretation #2 and the corresponding question. Point out that the questioner is opening the door to a dialogue that may present an answer he or she does not now know.

- Use slide 9–24 to explain the steps of the activity.

2. Work in pairs (10 minutes)

   - Direct participants to form pairs and read each of the six scenarios described in Training Instrument 13–12. They are to suggest possible explanations for each behavior observed and to devise nonjudgmental questions that would uncover reasons for each behavior. Call time after 10 minutes.

3. Debrief the experience (10 minutes)

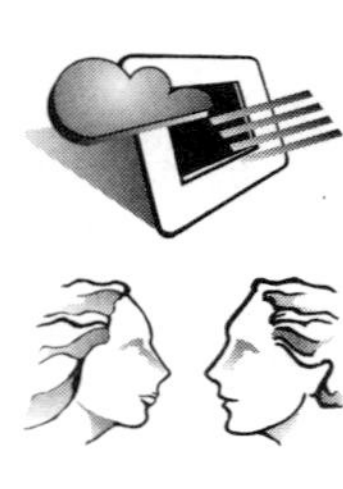

   - Display slide 9–25 and facilitate a group discussion of the questions presented there.

   - **An option:** You might have the small groups discuss the questions on slide 9–25 before the general debriefing. Remember to adjust the time accordingly if you choose this option: 10 minutes for the small-group discussion and 10 minutes for the large-group debriefing.

Learning Activity 12–10: Driver Portraits

Note: Only run this activity when you plan to follow it with Learning Activity 12–11: Disproving Stereotypes. Otherwise, you will be awakening stereotypes without disproving them, and that could cause more harm than good.

GOAL

The goal of this activity is to help participants become aware of their own stereotypes.

MATERIALS

- Tool 13–4: Vehicle Card Set (cut the pictures apart to create separate cards)
- Tool 13–5: Vehicle Cards Composite
- Training Instrument 13–13: Driver Portraits
- PowerPoint slides 10–5 and 10–6 (To access the slides for this learning activity, open the PowerPoint file *Module 3.ppt/pps* on the accompanying CD. Thumbnail copies of the slides are included at the end of chapter 10.)

TIME

- 35 minutes

INSTRUCTIONS

1. Introduce the exercise (5 minutes)
   - Display slide 10–5.
   - Distribute a copy of Training Instrument 13–13: Driver Portraits to each participant.
   - Explain that each group will receive two pictures of vehicles and they will have 10 minutes to fully describe the people who would be operating those vehicles.
   - Distribute two pictures to each group.
   - **Tip:** Introduce this exercise lightly, encouraging participants to have fun with it. If someone asks if she is supposed to stereotype

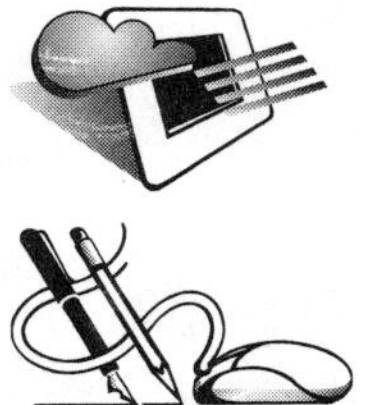

the drivers, try this answer: *Write whatever comes to mind when you look at these pictures. For now, don't worry about whether it's a stereotype.*

2. Participants create descriptions within their groups (10 minutes)

3. Groups share verbal portraits (10 minutes)

- Ask a representative from each group to share the group's driver descriptions with the full class.

- **Tip:** Before the large-group sharing, distribute pictures of all the vehicles (Tool 13–5: Vehicle Cards Composite) to each group so everyone will have a point of reference as they listen to other groups' descriptions. Or you might enlarge the pictures of the vehicles and post them on the walls around the room.

4. Debrief the experience (10 minutes)

- Display slide 10–6 and use the questions on the slide to facilitate a large-group discussion.
- Explain that these descriptions come from stereotypes, and that forming a stereotype is a normal human reaction. Humans form stereotypes as a way to simplify and make sense of a very complex world.

Learning Activity 12–11: Disproving Stereotypes

GOAL

The goal of this activity is to give participants practice in discarding old stereotypes when new and disproving information is introduced.

MATERIALS

- Training Instrument 13–14: Disproving Stereotypes
- PowerPoint slide 10–13 (To access the slide for this learning activity, open the PowerPoint file *Module 3.ppt/pps* on the accompanying CD. A thumbnail copy of the slide is included at the end of chapter 10.)

TIME

- 25 minutes

INSTRUCTIONS

1. Introduce the activity (5 minutes)

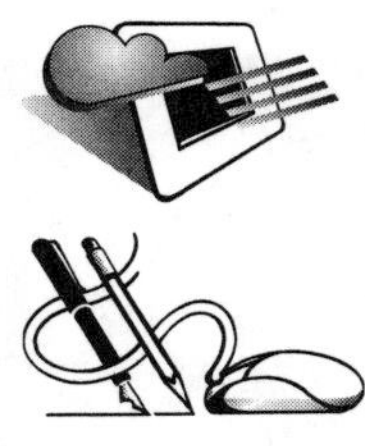

- Display slide 10–13.
- Distribute a copy of Training Instrument 13–14: Disproving Stereotypes to each participant.
- Ask each small group to elect a facilitator.

2. Small-group discussion (10 minutes)

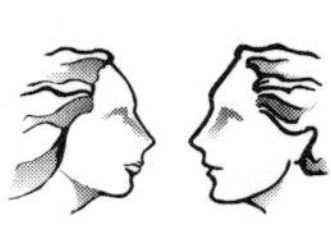

- Give groups 10 minutes to discuss the questions presented in the handout.

3. Debrief the experience (10 minutes)

- Have each group facilitator present the group's findings to the full class.
- Emphasize that the main problem is not the *presence* of stereotypes because their formation is a normal human reaction to a complex environment. The problem lies in stereotype rigidity, or the inability to change a stereotype when disproving information is given.

- **An interesting variation:** Substitute the vehicle pictures included in this book for pictures of vehicles owned by real people—perhaps even vehicles owned by company leaders. Then at the end of the activity you can reveal the owners of the vehicles and thus strengthen your stereotype-disproving message. Of course, make sure that the drivers and vehicles you select really disprove rather than prove existing stereotypes.

Learning Activity 12–12: How Old Were You?

GOAL

The goal of this activity is to help participants gain awareness of their own prejudices and connect them to life experiences and teachings.

MATERIALS

- Tool 13–6: Group Banners (Gather enough #10 envelopes so that each small group will have one. Cut the banners into separate strips and place one full set of banners into each envelope.)
- Training Instrument 13–15: How Old Were You?
- PowerPoint slides 11–4 through11–7 (To access the slides for this learning activity, open the PowerPoint file *Module 4.ppt/pps* on the accompanying CD. Thumbnail copies of the slides are included at the end of chapter 11.)

TIME

- 20 minutes

INSTRUCTIONS

1. Introduce the activity (5 minutes)

- Explain that often our attitudes toward certain groups are related to things we heard about them very early in our lives. Tell them that each person will have the opportunity to engage in some personal reflection on his or her attitudes toward a specific group and then to connect these attitudes to personal experiences and teachings related to that group.
- Distribute a copy of Training Instrument 13–15: How Old Were You? to each person.

- **Tip:** Reassure participants that whatever they write on the training instrument for this activity is for their eyes alone and will only be shared with others if they choose to do so.

- Display slide 11–4 and give each group an envelope containing a set of group banners (Tool 13–6). Tell each participant to pick one banner without looking inside the envelope.

2. Personal reflection (5 minutes)

- Ask participants to answer individually questions 1 through 3 in Training Instrument 13–15.

3. Pair discussion (5 minutes)

- Display slide 11–5.
- Invite participants to discuss their discoveries with one other person in the room.
- Reiterate that participants only need to share what they feel comfortable sharing. Suggest that during the pair discussion, participants focus on what they learned during their reflection and what they can do as a result of that learning rather than on specifics of their personal situation.

- **Key point:** Because there is a certain amount of risk associated with disclosing one's prejudices in the workplace, it is very important to emphasize that participants only need to share what they want to share. Suggest that participants keep their written comments confidential. If managers and employees are present in the same session, you may want to skip the dyad discussion altogether.
- **A variation:** Instead of inserting group banners into envelopes, simply pass around a list of groups and explain that each person is going to analyze what he or she was told or taught earlier in life about whichever group he or she selects from the list. You also may want to customize this activity by including in the list groups that are particularly relevant in your organization.

4. Conclusion (5 minutes)

- Display slide 11–6.
- Explain that prejudices are often subconscious attitudes with roots in early teachings from parents, teachers, and society.

- Display slide 11–7.

- Read the quote and emphasize that it is almost impossible not to have prejudices and that prejudices are often not rational decisions. It is important to constantly question our attitudes regarding other groups because these attitudes often influence our behaviors.

Learning Activity 12–13: A New Product Line

GOAL

The goal of this activity is to help participants make connections among stereotypes, prejudices, and decision making.

MATERIALS

- Tool 13–7: Candidate Information Cards (Cut sheets apart to produce separate cards. You will need one full set of cards for each group.)
- Training Instrument 13–16: A New Product Line
- Training Instrument 13–17: A New Product Line—Discussion Sheet
- PowerPoint slides 11–8 through 11–15 (To access the slides for this learning activity, open the PowerPoint file *Module 4.ppt/pps* on the accompanying CD. Thumbnail copies of the slides are included at the end of chapter 11.)

TIME

- 65 minutes

INSTRUCTIONS

1. Introduce the activity (10 minutes)

- Display slide 11–8.
- Explain that all participants are once again employees at the P^2C^2 Company. Each small group is one division. Tell them that they will select people to represent their divisions at headquarters. The opportunity to be the one division to produce a new product—gold paper clips—is at stake!

- Distribute Training Instrument 13–16. Instruct participants to read the full scenario, the slate of candidates, and the job description included in the handout. Give participants nine minutes to complete the reading.
- **Note:** You have two alternative means of presenting the details of this activity to the participants. You might choose to read the

material in Training Instrument 13–16 to the class. Or you might direct their attention to slides 11–9 through 11–12 for a summary of the details and then provide a separate list of candidates. Some participants prefer to be given detailed oral explanations by the facilitator. Others would rather read the information on their own. Some find slides more engaging than pages of text. How you present this material is your decision, and all modes are accommodated in this and many other activities in the workbook.

2. Make budget decisions (10 minutes)

- Tell participants they have 10 minutes to decide how to divide their budget. At the end of that time they must immediately send a representative to purchase any Candidate Information Cards (Tool 13–7) they have chosen.

- **Note:** Tell participants that Candidate Information Cards are available for a limited period of time. They must make a decision now or forfeit the opportunity to purchase information.

3. Make group selections (10 minutes)

- Tell participants they must now reach their final decisions on the people who will represent their divisions at headquarters. Explain that each group will have three to four minutes to present its team selection and the rationale behind its choice when the large group convenes.

- **Note:** Participants may argue that even after they purchase information cards, they still have insufficient information to make a decision. Explain that people frequently must make decisions based on incomplete information. Add that even thorough employment review processes often fail to reveal key aspects of a person's character, abilities, and general attitudes toward work.

4. Make group presentations (15 minutes)

- Display slide 11–13.

- Ask each group to present its decisions and the reasoning behind them to the full class.

5. Small-group discussions (10 minutes)

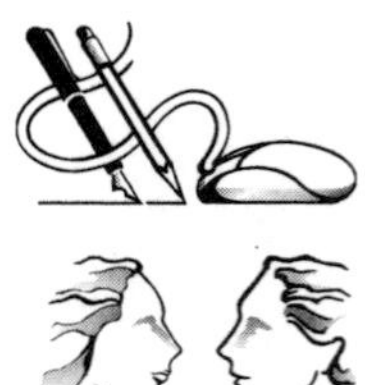

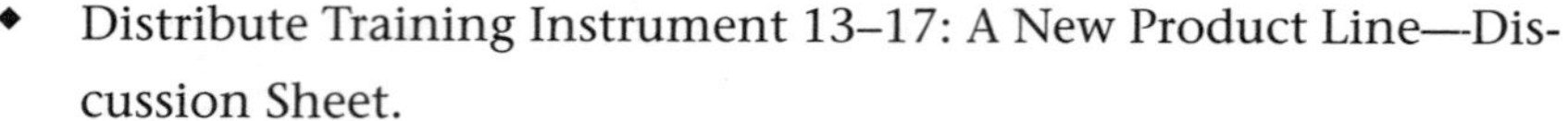

- Distribute Training Instrument 13–17: A New Product Line—Discussion Sheet.
- Ask each group to discuss the questions on the sheet and prepare to present its conclusions to the large group.
- **Tip:** You may find it helpful at this point to distribute to all participants copies of all of the character cards. Groups may then recognize the assumptions they made and reconsider previous decisions.

6. Debrief the experience (10 minutes)

- Facilitate a large-group discussion on the experience and the groups' conclusions.

- Use the quotes presented on slides 11–14 and 11–15 to explain that most people make assumptions based on incomplete information. Often these assumptions are predicated on stereotypes and on information received in very early years.

Learning Activity 12–14: The Company Picnic

GOAL

The goal of this activity is to help participants identify subtle discriminatory behaviors involving body language, tone of voice, eye contact, and so forth.

MATERIALS

- A deck of playing cards
- Training Instrument 13–18: The Company Picnic—Discussion Sheet
- PowerPoint slides 11–16 through 11–20 (To access the slides for this learning activity, open the PowerPoint file *Module 4.ppt/pps* on the accompanying CD. Thumbnail copies of the slides are included at the end of chapter 11.)
- Light refreshments

TIME

- 40 minutes

INSTRUCTIONS

When preparing for this training session, create a deck of cards equal in number to the number of participants in the class. Be sure to select only one Ace, and at least one King, one Queen, one Jack, one 3, and one 2 card. Fill out your deck by picking randomly from the numbers in between.

1. Introduce the activity (5 minutes)
    - Display slide 11–16.

    - Read or paraphrase the information on the slide.
    - Display slide 11–17.

    - Explain the ranks indicated by the cards.

The instructions for this activity were adapted from those developed by Sivasailam "Thiagi" Thiagarajan. Used with permission from the author.

- Distribute cards, one per participant, *making sure participants do not see their own cards*. Instruct them to hold their cards up to their foreheads, face out.
- Emphasize that participants must not look at their cards or tell each other what cards they have.
- As you give instructions, it is best not to tell participants how to treat people. Tell them to relate to one another the way they would normally if people really had the ranks indicated by the cards held to their foreheads. Otherwise, during the debriefing participants may argue that the facilitator told them to mistreat those with a low rank.

2. Enjoy the picnic (5 minutes)

- Encourage everyone to move around the room, get coffee or sodas, and just mingle as they would at a company picnic. Remind them to keep their cards close to their foreheads.

3. Form the picnic line (5 minutes)

- After five minutes of mingling, ask participants to form a line in rank order from the CEO (the Ace) to the lowest ranks (3s and 2s).
- Tell them not to look at their own cards but to position themselves according to their perceived rank (based on the way people treated them during the mingling). When the line is formed, ask participants to state their ranks. Only then let them see their cards.
- Instruct everyone to take their seats.

4. Small-group discussions (8 minutes)

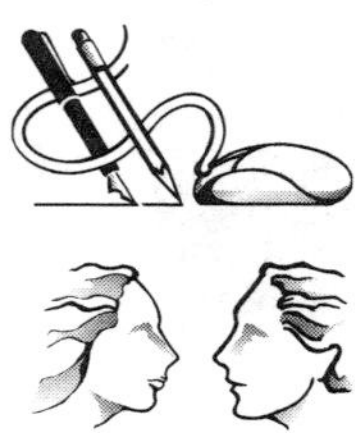

- Distribute Training Instrument 13–18: A Company Picnic—Discussion Sheet.
- Ask participants to answer questions in groups and prepare to report their findings to the large group.

5. Debrief the experience (7 minutes)

- Allow participants to report their findings.

- Display slide 11–18.

- Summarize the contents of the slide and emphasize that attitudes are connected to behaviors, and that people are able to perceive even subtle expressions of discrimination.

6. Brief discussion and lecture on subtle discrimination (10 minutes)

- Display slide 11–19.
- Ask participants for examples of subtle discrimination.

- Display slide 11–20.
- Read or paraphrase the content of the slide.
- **Note:** You may explain to participants that discriminatory behaviors are often more prevalent in informal and nonmandatory situations, such as after-work happy hours, weekend golf outings, or impromptu employee lunches. Although it is almost impossible to eliminate discrimination in those situations, they are nonetheless part of the overall employment experience and do affect employee satisfaction levels. They also may influence people's chances for success because mentoring and information gathering often happen in informal environments. Suggest that because discrimination is often subtle and the attitudes that cause it are typically subconscious, continuous learning and self-awareness are the only solutions.

Learning Activity 12–15: Subtle Discrimination

GOAL

The goal of this activity is to help participants discuss the impact of subtle discrimination in the workplace and devise an action plan to reduce it.

MATERIALS

- Training Instrument 13–19: Subtle Discrimination—Discussion Sheet
- PowerPoint slide 11–21 (To access the slide for this learning activity, open the PowerPoint file *Module 4.ppt/.pps* on the accompanying CD. A thumbnail copy of the slide is included at the end of chapter 11.)
- Flipchart paper, marking pens, magazines, scissors, glue or tape (optional)

TIME

- 10 minutes

INSTRUCTIONS

- Display slide 11–21.
- Distribute a copy of Training Instrument 13–19: Subtle Discrimination—Discussion Sheet to each participant.
- Have groups select a representative who will make notes of the discussion and report to the large group.

- Ask groups to discuss the questions on the handout (and the slide).
- Emphasize that the last question (What can you *do* about it?) is the most important one. Ask groups to come up with at least three positive actions they can take to reduce subtle discrimination.
- Ask each group representative to share the group's discussions and action plans with the whole class.
- **A concluding variation:** This variation of the exercise may serve well as a concluding activity for a workshop. Tell participants they

have received an award for having reduced subtle discrimination and improved work relationships. Have them develop a poster using flipchart paper, markers, and clippings from magazines to explain to the large group why they received the award.

Chapter 13

Training Instruments, Assessments, and Tools

What's in This Chapter?

- Materials to support your diversity development sessions, including two assessments, seven tools, and 19 training instruments

A time-consuming piece of instructional design is the development of training materials, including handouts, cards, game instructions, and the like. This chapter includes all the materials you need to successfully run the activities described in Modules 1–4 (chapters 8–11) and in chapter 12. With these materials prepared (and ready for customizing as needed), you will be able to focus your efforts on developing the business case for diversity at your own organization.

Using the CD

Materials included in this chapter are also available as electronic files on the accompanying CD. To access the electronic files, insert the CD and click on the appropriate Adobe .pdf documents. Further directions and help in locating and using the files can be found in the Appendix, "Using the Compact Disc" at the end of this workbook.

Training Instrument 13–1

Introducing Conversity

Conversity means

- engaging in conversation to discover connections
- allowing the similarities that bring us together to open us to the differences that enrich us.

What could be the payoff to discovering these similarities?

___

___

___

Instructions: Choose a partner and have a dialogue to find as many hidden similarities as possible. Go beyond the obvious and search for invisible similarities, such as aspirations, hopes, personality styles, hobbies, interests, fears, and so forth. In the space below, note the similarities you discover in the conversation.

Training Instrument 13–2

Next Steps

Instructions: With thought to the content of the program presented, answer the following questions. Your goal is to suggest some action steps that the organization's leadership can take to support a diversity development program.

1. Where do we go from here?

2. How will the leadership demonstrate its commitment to developing diversity in the organization?

Training Instrument 13–3

Welcome to P^2C^2

Scenario:

Congratulations! You are an employee of the world-renowned Platinum Paper Clip Company, or P^2C^2. At P^2C^2 paper clips are the most valuable commodity. Everything in your work life depends on your ability to accumulate paper clips—bonuses, rewards, even promotions. It's the end of P^2C^2's fiscal year and all teams are competing for the most important reward of the year: a full jar of paper clips! Your team must convince a panel of distinguished judges that it is deserving of this highest honor. Good luck and may the best team win "The Jar"!

Instructions: Working as a team, you have 10 minutes to complete the following two-part mission:

- Prepare a persuasive presentation explaining why your group deserves the jar of paper clips.
- Pick two team members to represent your group: one of them will serve on the panel of judges, the other will make the presentation to the panel.

Use the space below to make notes for your presentation and to record the names of your representatives and your rationale for choosing them.

Training Instrument 13–4

Windfall!

Scenario:

The board of directors at P^2C^2 has decided to award 20 additional paper clips as a bonus to the entire organization, and it has asked for suggestions on how best to make the distribution.

Instructions: Your team has five minutes to decide how to divide this windfall throughout the organization. Get ready to present and justify your solutions to the whole group. Your spokesperson will have one minute to make your case. Use the space below to devise your plan and explain your reasoning.

Training Instrument 13–5

The P^2C^2 Challenge

Instructions: As a group, discuss the following questions. Use the space provided to write your answers and those of other group members.

1. How did you form groups in the first place?

2. How did you feel about the panel decisions?

3. How did you decide on a paper clip distribution plan?

4. How does this experience relate to real life?

5. What did you learn?

Training Instrument 13–6

Personal Commitment Worksheet

Instructions: After a brief reflection, answer the following questions. Be precise in describing the actions you can and will take.

1. How can you apply what you learned today?

2. What is *one* thing you can do as a result of today's discussions?

Training Instrument 13–7

Group Brainstorm

Instructions: The goal here is to recall the lessons learned in the previous module. Write your answers in the spaces provided. Be as complete and descriptive in your answers as you can be. This will help enhance your learning.

1. What topics did we discuss in the previous module?

2. What are some practical workplace applications of what we discussed?

Training Instrument 13–8

The Interview

Scenario:

Your division at P^2C^2 is hiring a new team member. You are looking for someone with impeccable professionalism, a strong work ethic, and impressive leadership skills. The pool has been narrowed to three candidates.

Instructions: Choose one volunteer from the class to serve as the interviewer and three others to act as candidates. The entire class will be the hiring committee and will observe the three interviews. It's a good idea to take notes as you listen to the candidates: What do you like about each one? What don't you like? When all candidates have completed their interviews, discuss the following questions as a group:

1. What behaviors did you observe in each of the candidates?

A. Candidate #1:

B. Candidate #2:

C. Candidate #3:

2. What candidate would you choose, and why?

Training Instrument 13–9

Your Cultural Continuum

Culture deeply influences our values and behaviors—but it does not *prescribe* them. Individuals are still free to think, feel, and act in ways that are very different from their cultural norms.

Instructions: The lines below represent continua between two extremes for six cultural dimensions. Your goal is to place yourself and what you consider to be the average member of the U.S. culture somewhere along each continuum.

1. Assess your own preferences and place an **O** wherever appropriate along each line.
2. Ask yourself where a typical member of the predominant U.S. culture might place himself or herself along the continuum. Indicate that position with an **X**.
3. When you've completed all six dimensions, discuss your answers with your groups.

Communication preferences

Indirect, will beat around the bush before making a point ⟷ *Very direct, to the point, will tell it like it is*

Need for harmony, dislike of conflict

Conflict is very uncomfortable and should be avoided ⟷ *Conflict is fine; it is a way to reach better solutions*

Importance of punctuality

Punctuality is not very important; multitasking is fine; people are more important than time ⟷ *Punctuality is of great importance; it denotes respect for the person with whom you are dealing*

Equality between genders

Male and female roles are highly differentiated ⟷ *Males and females have equal roles in society*

Equality among people in general

Hierarchy and differentiation between people create order and comfort; people know where they stand ⟷ *All people are created equal; only achievements differentiate people*

Importance of relationships in business negotiations

Relationships are vital in business ⟷ *The quality of your services and products is more important than your relationship with clients*

Training Instrument 13–10
Value Congruency

Instructions: Imagine that values need to be funded and you have $15 to distribute among 10 of them. You do not have to divide the money evenly. For example, you may choose to pay $5 each for 3 values and ignore the other 7. The amount of money you assign to a value should match its importance. This exercise will be completed in three parts.

Part I: Personal Values. In column A indicate how you *personally* would distribute the $15 by placing an amount beside each of the values listed. Place a zero beside those values that you choose not to fund.

Part II: Organizational Values. *As a group,* consider what values are important to the organization and divide the money accordingly. The group *must reach consensus.* Voting is not allowed. Indicate the amounts for each value in column B.

Part III: Value Congruency. Value congruency is the contrast between your personal values and those of the organization you work for. In this exercise, your value congruency is the difference between the values in columns A and B. To identify this congruency, subtract the lower number from the higher number for each value and write it in column C. Don't bother with plus and minus; what is important is the degree of difference, not whether the difference is positive or negative.

	A	B	C
VALUE	HOW YOU RANK THIS VALUE	HOW THE ORGANIZATION RANKS THIS VALUE	VALUE CONGRUENCY
Balance between work and family			
Recognition			
Innovation			
Profits/compensation			
Continuous learning			
Community involvement			
Stability			
Integrity			
Diversity			
Equality			
Total			

Questions for Group Discussion

1. How do organizational/individual value congruency levels affect each of you?
2. How do value differences influence relationships among team members?
3. What can you do about it?

Training Instrument 13–11

Value Decision Making

Our values influence the decisions we make daily. What happens when a group needs to make a decision and it requires that all members agree?

For this exercise you will:

1. receive specific value instructions on individual cards
2. use the information on the value cards as a basis for everything you say during the exercise
3. reach a group decision via consensus, despite value differences.

Voting is not allowed as a means of arriving at a decision. You may use body language to express displeasure, as long as it is in keeping with the value instructions you receive. (**Tip**: Watch others!)

Scenario:

The P^2C^2 CEO is considering a new product line: platinum paper clips. P^2C^2 headquarters wants all divisions to supply market information as soon as possible. Your team has just been asked to put together an extensive market survey and to have the results ready by next Monday. Today is Thursday. To meet this deadline team members will need to contact clients and potential clients throughout the weekend.

Instructions: Discuss the following questions and arrive at consensus on the answers.

1. What should you say to headquarters?
2. What do you need to do to accomplish this task?
3. How will you divide the work among team members?

Training Instrument 13–12

Figuring Things Out

It's easy to interpret situations based on the way we see things through our own lenses—and then to assume that our interpretations are correct. But people's behaviors are most often inherently logical, even if we can't understand the logic behind them.

Scenario:

John, a team member, goes home exactly at 5 p.m. each evening. Everyone else stays longer, and a couple of team members work until 7 p.m. Some of you are upset with John and feel that he's not pulling his weight on the team.

> **Interpretation #1:** John is a slacker.
>
> *Question:* John, why aren't you willing to stay and help us out? We're getting tired of doing your work and we have lives outside this office, too!
>
> **Interpretation #2:** John has a logical reason for his behavior and you don't know that reason.
>
> *Question:* John, we seem to work at different times. Can we talk about that?

Instructions: Working with a partner, read each of the six scenarios described below. Try to come up with possible reasons for the behaviors expressed and take turns devising nonjudgmental questions. Write the questions in the spaces provided.

1. Maggie is a new hire and seems to express her disapproval of company procedures and policies frequently. Maggie's motto appears to be "If it ain't broke, let's break it." Her constant calls for change are driving you crazy.

2. Louis reports to you. You are frustrated because when he expresses a problem, he seldom brings a solution. You would like him to have more initiative.

Continued on next page

Training Instrument 13–12, continued

Figuring Things Out

3. Edward is such a stickler for detail! Just yesterday he sent back a report you had prepared, arguing that the typeface used didn't match the specifications of the company's image manual. You feel you don't have time for such petty stuff.

4. You were pleased with the way you presented the team report to management. Right after the presentation, however, Julia approached you in great distress. She felt her contributions to the team had been ignored. You don't understand Julia. Wasn't it supposed to be a team effort? Why can't she put her ego aside?

5. Jason is really quiet. He hardly ever speaks up during a meeting and you know he has some killer ideas. You feel he is lackadaisical and doesn't contribute enough to the team. Is he afraid to speak his mind?

6. Come up with your own situation. Was there ever a time in which a team member's behavior seemed completely illogical? Could culture or values have had anything to do with it?

Training Instrument 13–13

Driver Portraits

Instructions: Each group will receive pictures of two vehicles. As a group, decide the answers to the following questions. Make any assumptions you need to make to "create a life" for the drivers. Think about their hopes and dreams, family lives, hobbies, and professional experiences. Add any details that will help the full class know your drivers better.

1. Who drives or rides these vehicles?
2. What are their names and ethnicities?
3. Where do they work?
4. What are their educational levels?

Questions for Group Discussion

Instructions: As a group, discuss the following questions. Make notes on the answers suggested in the spaces provided.

1. How can you reduce stereotypes?

2. How can you apply Conversity techniques when reducing stereotypes?

3. How can you minimize the influence of stereotypes in decision making?

Training Instrument 13–14
Disproving Stereotypes

Instructions: As a group, discuss the following questions. Make notes on suggested answers in the spaces provided.

1. Who else could be driving these vehicles?

2. How can you disprove stereotypes? Bring up specific examples of people who disprove the stereotypes you used for the driver portraits.

Training Instrument 13–15

How Old Were You?

Instructions: Following a period of personal reflection, write in the name of the group you have selected and answer the questions below.

1. Group selected: ______________________________

2. How old were you when you first heard about this group? ______________

3. Indicate in the chart below what you heard about this group from your parents, peers, and other sources during the early phases of your life.

INFLUENCE	AGE 0–10 YEARS	AGE 11–18 YEARS
Parents		
Peers		
Other sources (teachers, other authority figures, the media)		

4. How did those teachings influence your thoughts and feelings about this group?

5. What can you do about it?

Training Instrument 13–16

A New Product Line

Scenario:

Great news! P^2C^2 headquarters has finally given the go ahead to an exciting new product line: gold paper clips. Your division is competing with others around the country to produce the new clips. Before the directors of P^2C^2 make a final decision, they want to hear a team of representatives from each division explain why their division should produce the clips.

Your job today is to select 5 representatives from a slate of 10 qualified candidates. There is only one problem: Because of a clerical error you were only given the following information on each candidate:

- name
- age
- group or groups with which the candidate is most commonly identified.

Additional information may be requested from the headquarters database, but there is a cost associated with the search and provision of those data.

Your division has $1,000 available so you must choose between the following options in making your decision:

- running a training session on a topic of your choice to prepare the selected team *and* obtaining additional information on two candidates only
- obtaining additional information on four candidates, and therefore having no money left for training.

Slate of Candidates:

1. Sam Walker, 35, white males, people with disabilities
2. Becky Morgan, 65, white females, GLBTs (gay/lesbian/bisexual/transgender people), older workers
3. Robert Santana, 42, Hispanic males
4. Kay Creek, 36, African-American females, single mothers
5. Ashid Allayah, 30, Muslim males, Generation-Xers
6. Bob Taylor, 42, white males, single parents
7. Alison Miller, 38, white females, accountants
8. Edward da Costa, 26, white males, Generation-Yers

Continued on next page

Training Instrument 13–16, continued

A New Product Line

9. Maria Alvarez-Edwards, 24, Hispanic females, Generation-Yers
10. Arthur Shorenstein, 67, Jewish males, Korean War veterans, older workers

Job Description for Division Representative:

The division representative must be able to

- work well in a team
- make a clear and compelling presentation to headquarters
- undertake the required travel.

Training Instrument 13–17

A New Product Line—Discussion Sheet

Instructions: Answer the following questions as a group. Make notes in the spaces provided.

1. How did you make your decisions?

2. What assumptions did you make?

3. What was the connection between stereotypes and decision making?

4. How does this relate to real life?

Training Instrument 13–18

The Company Picnic—Discussion Sheet

Instructions: Answer the following questions in the spaces provided.

1. How could you tell what your rank was?

2. How did you decide how to treat others?

3. Is this exercise "real"?

Training Instrument 13–19

Subtle Discrimination—Discussion Sheet

Instructions: Answer the following questions in the spaces provided.

1. Can any of us say we have no prejudices? Why or why not?

2. How does subtle discrimination affect others?

3. What difference does subtle discrimination make in the workplace?

4. What can you do about it?

Assessment 13–1

Diversity Self-Awareness

Instructions: Rate yourself for each statement on a scale of 1 to 5. Be open and honest with yourself. Put a checkmark in the appropriate box.

KEY: 1 = RARELY 3 = SOMETIMES 5 = ALWAYS

		1	2	3	4	5
1.	I recognize that there are many ways a person can experience discrimination.	☐	☐	☐	☐	☐
2.	I am aware of the main characteristics of my own culture.	☐	☐	☐	☐	☐
3.	I understand that words have historic connotations and I take the time to learn about labels that negatively affect specific groups of people.	☐	☐	☐	☐	☐
4.	I learn about the characteristics of different cultures in my organization.	☐	☐	☐	☐	☐
5.	I keep abreast of the latest legislative developments related to diversity management.	☐	☐	☐	☐	☐
6.	I read a diversity-related publication.	☐	☐	☐	☐	☐
7.	I ask questions and am curious about different people and customs.	☐	☐	☐	☐	☐
8.	I understand how culture influences attitudes and behaviors in the workplace.	☐	☐	☐	☐	☐
9.	I am aware of stereotypes I hold of other groups.	☐	☐	☐	☐	☐
10.	I am comfortable discussing diversity.	☐	☐	☐	☐	☐
11.	I am comfortable with foreign accents.	☐	☐	☐	☐	☐
12.	I enjoy working with people from different cultural backgrounds.	☐	☐	☐	☐	☐
13.	I relate to people easily.	☐	☐	☐	☐	☐
14.	I am willing to take on a diversity leadership role.	☐	☐	☐	☐	☐
15.	I am comfortable with situations that I don't totally understand.	☐	☐	☐	☐	☐
16.	I am comfortable taking risks.	☐	☐	☐	☐	☐
17.	I see people positively.	☐	☐	☐	☐	☐

Continued on next page

Assessment 13–1, continued

Diversity Self-Awareness

	1	2	3	4	5
18. I am flexible.	☐	☐	☐	☐	☐
19. I recognize people for their contributions.	☐	☐	☐	☐	☐
20. I treat people the way *they* want to be treated.	☐	☐	☐	☐	☐
21. I practice good listening skills.	☐	☐	☐	☐	☐
22. I give balanced and effective feedback.	☐	☐	☐	☐	☐
23. I am a good communicator.	☐	☐	☐	☐	☐
24. I listen patiently when talking to people with limited English skills.	☐	☐	☐	☐	☐
25. I take my own biases into consideration before I make a decision or act.	☐	☐	☐	☐	☐
26. I actively put myself "in people's shoes" before I act.	☐	☐	☐	☐	☐
27. I actively look for similarities between myself and my co-workers.	☐	☐	☐	☐	☐

BACKGROUND AND SCORING

A literature search conducted by Arash Afshar for an article titled "Competencies for All Differences" (ASTD et al., 1996) identified three basic diversity competency areas: knowledge (historical developments, causes of exclusion, cultural differences, and so forth), attitudes (warmth, empathy, willingness to affect the environment, flexibility), and skills (communications, conflict management, and the like). Other authors have referred to these basic areas as *head* (knowledge), *heart* (attitudes), and *hand* (behaviors and skills).

The statements you just read and responded to exemplify competencies in each of those three areas. Questions 1 through 9 refer to *head*, questions 10 through 18 refer to *heart*, and questions 19 through 27 refer to *hand*.

To determine your score, add up your numbers and write them in the second column of the table below.

	YOUR SCORE	MAXIMUM SCORE
Head questions 1–9		45
Heart questions 10–18		45
Hand questions 19–27		45
Total		**135**

Continued on next page

Assessment 13–1, continued

Diversity Self-Awareness

The three areas are interrelated. For instance, a low score on *Hand* might not necessarily indicate a lack of skill but an attitude of fear or unwillingness to take risks. It is helpful, therefore, to consider your entire score rather than the results in individual areas.

ACTION PLANS RELATED TO YOUR SCORE

If you scored low on Head, consider

- regularly reading a diversity publication such as the online items at Diversityinc.com or diversity articles published by the Society for Human Resource Management. Also check out the ASTD *Infoline* on diversity (Kamin, Wildermuth, and Collins, 2003).
- actively seeking people who are different from you and asking questions.
- studying legislative developments related to diversity.
- reading articles and publications on intercultural relations.

If you scored low on Heart, consider

- working on self-awareness and self-knowledge (consider workshops, instruments, self-help publications, and similar materials).
- asking yourself whether some of your discomfort could stem from personal experiences and fear of risk and failure (for instance, are you nervous about offending others?).
- actively "putting yourself in others' shoes" whenever possible.

If you scored low on Hand, consider

- actively working on your communication, conflict management, and leadership skills (through workshops, self-study, observation, coaching, and so forth).

It is helpful to seek support and coaching from other diversity leaders.

Assessment 13–2

Sample Level 1 Evaluation

Instructions: Please take a few minutes to let us know what you thought of the session today. Your answers will help us improve this training for future presentations.

1. What I liked most about today was

2. What I would change about this session is

3. I thought the instructor

4. In the future, what would help me on the job is

Tool 13–1
Interviewer Questions

Instructions: You will meet three candidates today. Here are the questions you will pose to each of them.

1. What important successes have you had in your career?
2. We encourage positive competition in our teams. Will you be comfortable in such an environment?
3. In a recent meeting, our CEO declared that between work and family life, work should take priority. The CEO believes that without work, you can't possibly support your family. How would you respond to this statement?

Tool 13–2
Cultural Rules Card Set

Facilitator instructions: Cut cards apart and give one card to each candidate.

Candidate 1's Cultural Rules

Your general behavior: Lively, animated, talkative

Do: Chit-chat before you establish rapport, talk about your family. Explain that you met your spouse when he or she reported to you at your previous job.

Do not: Compete. If you are asked questions about competition, make sure that the interviewer understands that you never compete with team members.

Candidate 2's Cultural Rules

Your general behavior: Calm, reserved, quiet

Do: Leave respectful pauses before responding to any questions (as long as 10 to 15 seconds).

Do not: Boast about personal success. Rather, somewhat downplay your achievements. The interviewer will understand you are being appropriately modest.

Candidate 3's Cultural Rules

Your general behavior: Assertive and enthusiastic

Do: Talk about your accomplishments; compete with others fairly.

Do not: Mix family and work life; hire or give preference to relatives at work; ask the boss to make all decisions. Make sure you let the interviewer know how you feel about those issues.

Tool 13–3
Values Card Set

Facilitator instructions: Make one copy of this card set for each group. Cut cards apart and distribute a complete set of cards to each group.

Value Card 1

Your key value: Balance between work and family life

You believe that there is time for work and time for family, and the two should not interfere with one another. You have three kids and feel you don't spend enough time with them. They are your first and foremost priority.

Value Card 2

Your key value: Personal space

You are introverted and need to rewind on weekends by spending some time alone. You are against disturbing people on weekends and feel that all work should be done during the week. You also have strong opinions about calling people at their homes, believing that a person's home should be sacred.

Value Card 3

Your key value: Productivity

You feel a lot of loyalty to your organization and believe that there is little the organization could ask of you that you wouldn't do. You believe hard work is essential in life and nothing can be achieved without considerable effort and sacrifice.

Continued on next page

Tool 13–3, continued

Values Card Set

Value Card 4

Your key value: Flexibility

You feel there is always a solution to any problem if only people will be flexible. You are always willing to change your hours to accommodate work needs, as long as the organization is flexible with you when needed.

Value Card 5

Your key values: Spirituality and community involvement

Weekends are important for you. You spend them with your family, volunteer at your place of worship, and help in your community. You believe two days out of seven is already a small contribution and will resist any suggestions to work on those days.

Value Card 6

Your key value: Recognition

You don't mind working until the wee hours if needed, but you want to make absolutely sure your contributions are valued, recognized, and rewarded.

Tool 13–4

Vehicle Card Set

Facilitator instructions: Cut out each vehicle card and distribute two cards to each group.

3

5

6

Continued on next page

Tool 13–4, continued

Vehicle Card Set

7

8

9

10

Tool 13–5

Vehicle Cards Composite Sheet

Facilitator instructions: Print one composite sheet for each group. Distribute the composite sheets during the debriefing.

1

2

3

4

5

6

7

8

9

10

Tool 13–6
Group Banners

Facilitator instructions: Make one copy of this tool and get one #10 envelope for each group. Cut the banners into sets and place one set in each envelope. Give one envelope to each group and have all participants select one banner from the envelope.

ASIAN AMERICANS

CAUCASIAN AMERICANS

ELDERLY PEOPLE

EXTREMELY OVERWEIGHT PEOPLE

FOREIGN IMMIGRANTS

HISPANIC AMERICANS

INSURANCE SALESPEOPLE

JEWS

MUSLIMS

NATIVE AMERICANS

OLDER WORKERS

SINGLE PARENTS

USED-CAR SALESPEOPLE

Tool 13–7
Candidate Information Cards

Facilitator instructions: Make one copy of all the cards for each small group. Cut the cards apart, keeping them in sets. If requested, give appropriate cards to group representatives.

1. People with Disabilities

Name: Sam Walker

Age: 35

Brief Description: Paraplegic as a result of a car accident in his youth. Lives on his own, no family. He is currently looking for another job.

Strengths: High energy, enthusiastic; long list of previous jobs; highly experienced in his field of expertise

Weaknesses: Perceived as withdrawn; needs long time to process and reflect on information

2. Gay, Lesbian, Bisexual, and Transgender People

Name: Becky Morgan

Age: 65

Brief Description: Is openly gay and has a life-partner of 36 years. Is close to her 16 nieces and nephews. Has worked for the company for 30 years.

Strengths: Strong leader; clear vision; gets the job done

Weaknesses: Needs to better delegate to meet timeline demands

3. Hispanics

Name: Robert Santana

Age: 42

Brief Description: Married with family; has two children; lives 1.5 hours away from work location.

Strengths: Excellent team-building leadership skills; has worked with people from numerous cultures and backgrounds

Weaknesses: Low tolerance for others who are not open-minded; needs to increase acceptance of others; has tremendous stage fright

Continued on next page

Tool 13–7, continued

Candidate Information Cards

4. Blacks

Name: Kay Creek

Age: 36

Brief Description: Single mother of two schoolage children; one child has Down's Syndrome.

Strengths: Has excellent employee relations skills; is an advocate for employees; knows how to promote problem-solving skills with leaders

Weaknesses: High expectations of others to lead with excellence; expects more from people who do not have the skills

5. Muslims

Name: Ashid Allayah

Age: 27

Brief Description: Pillar of his community; willing to lend a helping hand to others; considered extremely handsome; was promoted three times within the last five years.

Strengths: Always willing to help others in the workplace

Weaknesses: Time management to complete his responsibilities; not openly supportive of changes in the workplace

6. Single Parents

Name: Bob Taylor

Age: 42

Brief Description: Widowed father of two young children who has worked for P^2C^2 for the last five years.

Strengths: Highly energetic; able to make friends easily; able to connect with people different from himself; is likely to make a good impression

Weaknesses: Not good with details; gets flustered with financial explanations; may be perceived as overselling your division

Continued on next page

Tool 13–7, continued

Candidate Information Cards

7. Accountants

Name: Alison Miller

Age: 48

Brief Description: Has worked for P^2C^2 for 10 years. She is loyal to the organization and jokingly says she is "married" to her job.

Strengths: Highly analytical; able to observe details that are often missed by others

Weaknesses: Was married to one of the key people at headquarters and still holds a grudge; rather narrow-minded and uncomfortable with lively negotiations

8. Salespeople

Name: Edward da Costa

Age: 26

Brief Description: A quiet young man with a strong interest in history and archaeology. He is known for his loyalty to the company and for his keen intelligence. His sales success is mostly attributable to his ability to develop long-term relationships with customers.

Strengths: Loyal; perceptive; excellent team player; able to foster a sense of harmony within the group

Weaknesses: Somewhat shy; strongly dislikes conflict; prefers one-to-one contact over large group discussions

9. New graduates

Name: Maria Alvarez-Edwards

Age: 24

Brief Description: Recently hired by P^2C^2 after interning with the company throughout her junior and senior years in P^2C^2's summer internship programs.

Strengths: Relates well with all ages; has proven her ability to work well as a team member; has leadership skills

Weaknesses: Hasn't participated in many high-level discussions; needs to acquire more business savvy

Continued on next page

Tool 13–7, continued

Candidate Information Cards

10. People of Retirement Age

Name: Arthur Shorenstein

Age: 67

Brief Description: Arthur is a happy-go-lucky person who typically gets his way through influencing others. He has worked for P^2C^2 for the last two years and has been promoted twice within that period of time.

Strengths: Friendly; engaging; charismatic; gives the impression of genuine care for others

Weaknesses: Needs to learn to be more succinct and less talkative; oversells

Appendix

Using the Compact Disc

Insert the CD and locate the file *How to Use This CD.doc.*

Contents of the CD

The compact disc that accompanies this workbook on diversity training contains three types of files. All of the files can be used on a variety of computer platforms.

- **Adobe .pdf documents.** These include assessments, tools, and training instruments.
- **Microsoft PowerPoint presentations.** These presentations add interest and depth to many of the training activities included in the workbook.
- **Microsoft PowerPoint files of overhead transparency masters.** These files makes it easy to print viewgraphs and handouts in black-and-white rather than using an office copier. They contain only text and line drawings; there are no images to print in grayscale.

Computer Requirements

To read or print the .pdf files on the CD, you must have Adobe Acrobat Reader software installed on your system. The program can be downloaded free of cost from the Adobe Website, *www.adobe.com.*

To use or adapt the contents of the PowerPoint presentation files on the CD, you must have Microsoft PowerPoint software installed on your system. If you simply want to view the PowerPoint documents, you must have an appropriate viewer installed on your system. Microsoft provides various viewers free for downloading from its Website, *www.microsoft.com.*

Printing From the CD

TEXT FILES

You can print the training materials using Adobe Acrobat Reader. Simply open the .pdf file and print as many copies as you need. The following .pdf documents can be directly printed from the CD:

- Assessment 13–1: Diversity Self-Awareness
- Assessment 13–2: Sample Level 1 Evaluation
- Tool 13–1: Interviewer Questions
- Tool 13–2: Cultural Rules Card Set
- Tool 13–3: Values Card Set
- Tool 13–4: Vehicle Card Set
- Tool 13–5: Vehicle Cards Composite
- Tool 13–6: Group Banners
- Tool 13–7: Candidate Information Cards.
- Training Instrument 13–1: Introducing Conversity
- Training Instrument 13–2: Next Steps
- Training Instrument 13–3: Welcome to P^2C^2
- Training Instrument 13–4: Windfall!
- Training Instrument 13–5: The P^2C^2 Challenge
- Training Instrument 13–6: Personal Commitment Worksheet
- Training Instrument 13–7: Group Brainstorm
- Training Instrument 13–8: The Interview
- Training Instrument 13–9: Your Cultural Continuum
- Training Instrument 13–10: Value Congruency
- Training Instrument 13–11: Value Decision Making
- Training Instrument 13–12: Figuring Things Out
- Training Instrument 13–13: Driver Portraits
- Training Instrument 13–14: Disproving Stereotypes
- Training Instrument 13–15: How Old Were You?
- Training Instrument 13–16: A New Product Line
- Training Instrument 13–17: A New Product Line–Discussion Sheet

- Training Instrument 13–18: A Company Picnic—Discussion Sheet
- Training Instrument 13–19: Subtle Discrimination—Discussion Sheet

POWERPOINT SLIDES

You can print the presentation slides directly from this CD using Microsoft PowerPoint. Simply open the .ppt files and print as many copies as you need. You can also make handouts of the presentations by printing three "slides" per page. These slides will be in color, with design elements embedded. PowerPoint also permits you to print these in grayscale or black-and-white, although printing from the overhead masters file will yield better black-and-white representations. Many trainers who use personal computers to project their presentations bring along viewgraphs just in case there are glitches in the system. The overhead masters can be printed from the PowerPoint .pps files.

Adapting the PowerPoint Slides

You can modify or otherwise customize the slides by opening and editing them in the appropriate application. However, you must retain the denotation of the original source of the material—it is illegal to pass it off as your own work. You may indicate that a document was adapted from this workbook, written by Cris Wildermuth and Susan Gray and copyrighted by ASTD and Cris Wildermuth. The files will open as "Read Only," so before you adapt them you will need to save them onto your hard drive under a different file name.

Showing the PowerPoint Presentations

On the CD, the following PowerPoint presentations are included:

- Leadership.ppt
- Module 1.ppt
- Module 2.ppt
- Module 3.ppt
- Module 4.ppt

Having the presentations in .ppt format means that they automatically show full-screen when you double-click on a file name. You also can open Microsoft PowerPoint and launch the presentations from there.

Use the space bar, the enter key, or mouse clicks to advance through a show. Press the backspace key to back up. Use the escape key to abort a presentation.

Table A–1
Navigating Through a PowerPoint Presentation

KEY	POWERPOINT "SHOW" ACTION
Space bar *or* Enter *or* Mouse click	Advance through custom animations embedded in the presentation
Backspace	Back up to the last projected element of the presentation
Escape	Abort the presentation
B *or* b	Blank the screen to black
B *or* b *(repeat)*	Resume the presentation
W *or* w	Blank the screen to white
W *or* w *(repeat)*	Resume the presentation

If you want to blank the screen to black while the group discusses a point, press the B key. Pressing it again restores the show. If you want to blank the screen to a white background, do the same with the W key. Table A–1 summarizes these instructions.

We strongly recommend that trainers practice making presentations with the PowerPoint slides before using them in live training situations. You should be confident that you can cogently expand on the points featured in the presentations and discuss the methods for working through them. If you want to engage your training participants fully (rather than worrying about how to show the next slide), become familiar with this simple technology *before* you need to use it. A good practice is to insert notes into the *Speaker's Notes* feature of the PowerPoint program, print them out, and have them in front of you when you present the slides.

For Further Reading

Amalfe, C., and H. Akawie. (2004). *Diversity in the Workplace: The Benefits and Shortcomings of Internal Audits and Surveys*. 2004. Available at http://www.acca.com/public/article/diversity/oc.html.

Arbinger Institute. *Leadership and Self-Deception: Getting Out of the Box*. San Francisco: Berrett-Koehler Publishers, 2000.

ASTD, Disabilities Awareness Network, Sexual Orientation Issues in the Workplace Network, and Women's Network. *Elements of Competence for Diversity Work: Creating Competence for Inclusive Work Environments*. Alexandria, VA: ASTD.

Bamshad, M., and S. Olson. Does Race Exist? *Scientific American* 289 (6): 78–85.

Bennett, M. J. Towards Ethnorelativism: A Developmental Model of Intercultural Sensitivity. In *Education for the Intercultural Experience,* R. M. Paige, ed. Yarmouth, ME: Intercultural Press, 1993.

Brown, R. *Prejudice: Its Social Psychology*. Oxford, UK: Blackwell, 1995.

Cox, T. Jr. *Creating the Multicultural Organization: A Strategy for Capturing the Power of Diversity*. San Francisco: Jossey-Bass, 2001.

Delikat, M. The Legal Dangers in Diversity. *Corporate Board* 16 (91): 11–17.

De Palma, D. A. *Business Without Borders: A Strategic Guide to Global Marketing*. New York: John Wiley & Sons, 2002.

Duckitt, J. *The Social Psychology of Prejudice*. Westport, CT: Praeger, 1994.

Eichenwald, K. Texaco to Make Record Payout in Bias Lawsuit. *New York Times,*November 18, 1996, p. 1-1.

Gardenswartz, L, and A. Rowe. *The Managing Diversity Survival Guide*. Boston: McGraw-Hill, 1994.

Grensing-Pophal, L. A Balancing Act on Diversity Audits. *HR Magazine* 46 (11): 87–92.

Hammond, S. *The Thin Book of Appreciative Inquiry.* Bend, OR: Thin Book Publishing, 1998.

Hofstede, G. *Culture and Organizations: Software of the Mind.* New York: McGraw-Hill, 1997.

Holladay, C. L., J. L. Knight, D. L. Paige, and M. A. Quiñones The Influence of Framing on Attitudes Toward Diversity Training. *Human Resource Development Quarterly* 14 (3): 245–63.

Inscape Publishing. *Discovering Diversity Profile.* Minneapolis, MN: Author, 1994.

Kamin, M., C. Wildermuth, and R. Collins. Diversity Programs That Work. *Infoline* No. 250312. Alexandria, VA: ASTD.

Kirkpatrick, D., compiler. *Another Look at Evaluating Training Programs.* Alexandria, VA: ASTD, 1998.

Knuckey, J., and B. D'Andra Orey. Symbolic Racism. *Social Science Quarterly* 181 (4): 1027–36.

Kochan, T., K. Bezrukova, R. Ely, et al. *The Effects of Diversity on Business Performance: Report of the Diversity Research Network. 2002.* Available at http://66.102.7.104/search?hl=en&ie=UTF-8&q=cache:SBRFenztVHIJ:faculty.haas.berkeley.edu/levine/&spell=1.

Kohls, L. R. Intercultural Training for Overseas Posting. In *Training Know-how for Cross-Cultural and Diversity Trainers,* L. R. Kohls with H. L. Brussow, eds. Duncanville, TX: Adult Learning Systems, 1995.

Kohls, L. R., and J. Knight. *Developing Intercultural Awareness,* 2nd edition. Yarmouth, ME: Intercultural Press, 1994.

Myers, S. and J. Lambert. *Diversity Icebreakers.* Amherst, MA: Amherst Educational Publishing, 1994.

Prince, M. Anti-discrimination Training Useful to Prevent Bias Claims. *Business Insurance* 37 (4): 12.

Sabath, A. M. *International Business Etiquette: Latin America.* Franklin Lakes, NJ: Career Press, 2000.

Segal, J. Diversity Danger Zones. *HR Magazine* 40 (6): 31–38.

Stewart, E., and M. Bennett. *American Cultural Patterns: A Cross Cultural Perspective.* Yarmouth, ME: Intercultural Press, 1991.

Storti, C. *Americans at Work: A Guide to the Can-Do People.* Yarmouth, ME: Intercultural Press, 2004.

Sullivan, J. *The Future of Corporate Globalization.* Westport, CT: Quorum Books, 2002.

Summerfield, E. *Survival Kit for Multicultural Living.* Yarmouth, ME: Intercultural Press, 1997.

Thiagajaram, S., and B. Steinwachs. *Barnga: A Simulation Game on Cultural Clashes.* Yarmouth, ME: Intercultural Press, 1990.

Thomas, D., and R. Ely. Making Differences Matter. *Harvard Business Review* 74 (5): 79–91.

Trepagnier, B. Deconstructing Categories: The Exposure of Silent Racism. *Symbolic Interaction* 24 (2): 141–64.

Von Bergen, C. W., B. Soper, and T. Foster. Unintended Negative Effects of Diversity Management. *Public Personnel Management* 31 (2): 239–52.

Wildermuth, C. Research Connections in Diversity Development. Unpublished manuscript, 2004.

Wildermuth, C., and S. Gray. Diversity Development Competencies at Individual, Team, and Leadership Levels. Unpublished manuscript, 2004.

Willmore, J. The Seven (Actually Nine) Deadly Sins of New Performance Consultants. *T&D* 57 (8): 28–33.

USEFUL WEB PAGES

Cyborlink: www.cyborlink.com

Diversity site with information on various diversity-related topics, including culture, race, gender, disability, and others

Diversityinc.com: www.diversityinc.com

Executive Planet: www.executiveplanet.com

Information on business etiquette and culture from a variety of countries

Society for Human Resources Management (SHRM): www.shrm.org

Statistical and labor market information, demographic business case

U.S. Census Bureau: www.census.gov

Articles on diversity and human resources

About the Authors

Cristina de Mello e Souza Wildermuth, MEd, a native of Rio de Janeiro, Brazil, has had a varied career spanning more than 15 years in management, training, and education. Early in her career she adapted Xerox's sales training programs to the Brazilian culture and facilitated marketing and management programs for Brazilian and multinational corporations such as Petrobrás (Brazil's main oil company), Xerox, and IBM. Later she reorganized a literacy agency that represented such major U.S. publishers as Hyperion, Harper Collins, and Random House in Brazil.

After immigrating to the United States in 1992, Wildermuth completed a master's degree in training and development at Bowling Green State University (Ohio) and is working on a doctorate in leadership studies there now. She speaks four languages (English, Spanish, Portuguese, and French) and has made presentations at various national and international conferences, such as those sponsored by ASTD and by the Society for Intercultural Training. Wildermuth has held various board positions for the Dayton, Ohio, chapter of ASTD and will be vice president of communications in 2005. She served as general vice president of the Lima, Ohio, satellite chapter for two years. She lives in Cridersville, Ohio, with her husband Mel, her daughter Marguerite, and two dogs who—not having grasped the concept of good diversity relations—fight nonstop.

Over the last 20 years, **Susan D. Gray, PHR,** has been helping organizations, teams, and individuals define and achieve their desired goals. With a keen sensitivity to underlying human resource issues that are barriers to organizational effectiveness and team development, she focuses on elevating respectful interactions among all individuals in an organization and promoting team development at all levels, starting with self-awareness and skill enhancement. Gray has designed and delivered a range of human resource development interventions in both the public and private sectors in fields such as healthcare, hospitality, retail, financial services, manufacturing, and technology.

Deeply committed to community leadership, she served on the board of the Greater Cincinnati Human Resources Association (GCHRA) as diversity co-chair; on the program design committee for the Greater Cincinnati chapter of ASTD (GCASTD), GCHRA, and Northern Kentucky Human Resources Association; as program developer and presenter for GCASTD's training day conference for not-for-profit organizations; and on the design planning committee for the "Can We Talk?" initiative sponsored by the Black Career Women's Association. Currently Gray is pursuing a master's degree in industrial/organizational psychology through Capella University.

Notes

Notes

Notes

Notes